Tri-Valley Trails

**Hiking adventures in the greater
Livermore, Amador and
San Ramon valleys**

*Over 65 hikes in 10 parks within 30 minutes
of the Tri-Valley*

Nancy Rodrigue and Jacky Poulsen

Photography by Barbara Mallon

First edition October 2010

All photos by Barbara Mallon

Front cover photo: Del Valle Regional Park
Back cover photo: Morgan Territory Regional Preserve

Dedicated to the
Livermore Hillhikers
for their encouragement, support and
friendship

Tri-Valley Trails
Table of Contents

Tri-Valley Trails

"The mountains are calling and I must go."

John Muir

Introduction

The Tri-Valley, in the southeast part of the East Bay, is a special place for hikers. Select a vantage point in the center of the valley, somewhere between Livermore, Pleasanton and Dublin, and turn around slowly; a circle of low mountains is visible. Most of this circle of mountains is a part of the largest regional/municipal park system in the country. It is a destination spot for the entire bay region, not just Tri-Valley locals, as the terrain is spectacular and the views outstanding. The wide range of native flora, trees and wildlife is bountiful. Opportunities for hiking are endless on well-established trails or cross-country.

The authors have been hiking these trails for over 15 years, slowly building a repertoire of the best hikes. We are often asked, "What got you started?" The answer is simple; we wanted to explore the beauty in the hills surrounding us. We realized that the valley floor was only a part of our home. So, what's in the hills? It only took a couple of hikes to discover what we had been missing, so we kept going. Then we decided to share our discovery with the community in the form of this book.

So, who should hike? People of all ages and all sizes! The trails in this book are arranged from easy to challenging, so anyone can get started right now! The benefits of hiking will gradually reveal themselves to you, and you will be hooked. What some people may not realize is how soothing nature can be. Even a short walk away from civilization relieves stress, as the mind becomes preoccupied with the beauty of nature.

The Tri-Valley trails weave through a mosaic of extensive oak woodlands and annual grasslands mixed with seasonal wetlands, creeks, and streams. These natural habitats host a variety of native wildlife species including fox, elk,

1

bobcat, deer and coyote. The bright yellow of orioles and meadowlark, and the daunting size of golden eagles and red tail hawks will astound you. If it is your lucky day, bald eagles will embolden themselves and come out of hiding at Del Valle.

The wildflowers begin blooming in February and continue into the summer. They come in all colors and are abundant in this region. Expect to see fields of Chinese houses, shooting stars, lupine, California poppy, to name a few. Native trees are not only awesome and varied, they provide shade for sunny day hikes. Many, such as big leaf maple and sycamore, grow along the creeks and glow with color in the fall.

All of the hikes in this book are unique and differ from each other in views, vegetation, landform, and difficulty. However, they all share some common features typical of Northern California ecosystems. Expect to see lots of grassland, ponds, creeks, native trees, chaparral, rock formations, and sweeping views of the San Francisco Bay, the Sierra Nevada, Mt. Diablo, and the Central Valley. Large wildlife and snakes tend to be nocturnal or reclusive and are rarely seen. Avian enthusiasts, however, will be well rewarded. There is something for everyone!

Many new hikers are daunted by the hills. Our advice is to begin on the trails we label flat and then move up to easy, moderate and then strenuous, progressing at your own pace. It might take three months of hiking once or twice a week to feel comfortable in the moderate category, but this depends on your conditioning and how consistent it has been over your lifetime. Now is the time to get started so head to the hills!

Most of the trailheads in this book are within about a half hour of the two freeways that intersect the Tri Valley, Interstate 580 and 680. When planning a hike, consider the distance to the trailhead as well as the length of the hike. Most of the hikes in this book can be walked in under 4 hours.

We think you will be impressed with these trails and soon become avid hikers like us. What used to be exclusive ranch land and old homesteads is now available to everyone. Ranching is still evident in the parks (lots of grazing cattle) adding to the rural experience. The cows are usually friendly as long as you don't come between them and their calves, and will "moo" a welcome to you. We are all the owners of these parks so come take a look at your investment!

Happy trails!

Tri-Valley Parks Overview Map

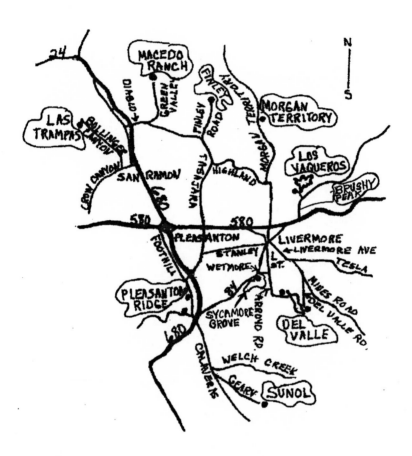

- Dots show approximate park entrance

Drawing around park names does not represent actual shape of park

This map is to provide a general idea of park locations and is not to scale.

How to Use this Book

The organization of this book makes it easy for you to find a hike that matches your hiking level and interests. The "Hikes By Attraction" section identifies some hikes that might be of particular interest. We encourage you to use this section to find the perfect hike for you!

There are ten parks represented in the book. Individual hikes are sequenced by difficulty level within each park, starting with the easiest. The parks themselves are sequenced alphabetically. Each park starts with an overview section, a map, and directions to the park entrance(s).

Individual hike write-ups include several sections: "Highlights" lists special features of the hikes, "Trail Details" outlines the distance, time and altitude gain for the hike, and "Getting There" describes which park entrance to use. "The Trail" describes the hike and gives detailed directions. A difficulty scale in the upper left corner provides a quick way for you to find a hike at the right level.

The scale, with the letters F-E-M-S (flat, easy, moderate, strenuous), has an arrow pointing to the difficulty level of the hike. A combination of total altitude gain, length of trail, length/climb ratio, steepness and condition of the trail are used to determine the placement of the arrow. Even with these details, the rating is somewhat subjective. Our advice is to hike a couple of hikes in this book and calibrate your skills to our ratings. Once you have a feel for what we mean by each level, you will find that the recommendations are consistent.

Difficulty Scale

The difficulty scale used in this book is a guideline to help you choose an appropriate hike for your hiking ability. An arrow points to the difficulty rating.

F__E_____M_____S

↑

Flat (F)-Up to 100' total altitude gain. These are often the shorter hikes.

Easy (E)-Approximately 100 to 500' total altitude gain. The trail has very gradual ups and downs.

Moderate (M)-Approximately 500' to 1500' total altitude gain. These trails are typically 4 to 6 miles with climbs that are spread out over the length of the hike.

Strenuous (S)-Typically more than 1500' total altitude gain spanning 6-10 miles, or several steep climbs and steep descents over a shorter distance. Particularly difficult hikes are indicated by an arrow to the right of the 'S'.

Book Terminology
Time
This is subjective and depends on the hiker's walking speed and the number of rests. In general, we base this on 25-minute miles with no rests. But climbing tends to be slower than descending. After you take one or two hikes, you can calibrate your own speed.

Distance
This is the approximate length of the entire hike.

Altitude Gain
This term describes the total cumulative elevation gain of the hike. All of the ascents are added together to determine this figure. Note that this is not the same as the difference between the elevation at the starting point and that of the highest point in

the hike. We provide this information as a guide; these figures are not intended to be exact. They can vary due to different measurement tools and rounding.

Highlights
These are the reasons we think you should take this hike, the things that make it special.

Getting there
This indicates where to park to get to the trailhead. Directions to the parking areas are in the park overview section for each park. All directions start at the intersection of Highways 580 and 680.

Option
Some hikes have options to alter, extend or shorten the hikes that are described in the write-ups but are not reflected in the numbers in the 'Trail Details' section.

Maps
Our maps are hand drawn by artistic license and are intended to be a guide. They are not exactly to scale. We strongly advise you to take along the free official trail maps that are often located in a box at most major park entrances. You can also download East Bay Regional Park District maps from their website at www.ebparks.org. Each hike indicates which trail map to use.

The maps in this book show the trails associated with the hike, but they do not name other neighboring trails. Keep in mind that trails, signs, outhouses and other markers change over time.

A few symbols are used: small circle for a pond, square for a structure, double hashes for a bridge. Two single hash lines with a horizontal line across the trail indicate a gate.

One caution: it is very easy to get disoriented! Always orient yourself before you start each hike. Look around for a landmark and determine what direction it is relative to the parking. For example, if you are at Los Vaqueros, note the direction of the lake. If you're at Morgan Territory, note the direction of Mt. Diablo. Better yet, carry a compass or GPS.

Practical Ideas for Safe/Successful Hiking

Weather: The Tri-Valley is perfect for year around hiking with some precautions. Summer temperature can exceed 100 degrees. At this time of year, it's best to hike in the morning when the cool evening air still lingers. Choose trails with tree cover or with trees on the east side that block the morning sun. Carry plenty of water for you and your pet and wear light colored, breathable fabric. Some trails dry out and become very dusty especially if shared with cows, horses and bikes. This only becomes a problem on steep down hill treks where they can be slippery.

Winter coolness and rain can come as early as mid-October or as late as the end of November. Typical daytime temperatures in winter range from the low 50's to the low 60's and can be windy. Rain turns the golden hills a luscious Kelly green. After a heavy rain, quite a few of the trails are muddy and sticky with wet clay. This can add a few pounds to your feet, so it might be best to avoid hiking for a couple of days.

What to wear: Weather can change during the course of a hike, so it's always best to bring layers. Lightweight hiking pants that can unzip into shorts are wonderful, especially in the spring and fall. Comfortable shoes with good tread are particularly important on hikes with climbs. Wear good hiking socks that won't cause blisters. On hot or sunny days a lightweight hat with a good visor is a must..

What to bring: Be sure to bring sunscreen, sunglasses, a hat and plenty of water. Do not plan to drink water from the streams along the trails as they are often contaminated. It's a good idea to have a compass or GPS, and always carry a park map. Hiking poles can be helpful especially if you have back or knee problems.

Wildlife: It is always a special treat to see animals in the wild. Sightings of large cats, elk, and boar are rare, especially in mid-day. Deer sightings are fairly common and always exciting. Once we saw a small herd of deer at Del Valle being stalked, then chased, by a bobcat. Luckily for the deer, our interruption sidetracked the chase. It's a good idea to be a noisy hiker so the animals get a warning to bolt, avoiding a confrontation with humans.

Cows graze in many of the parks. Keep your distance when calves are nearby, as the moms are very protective of their young.

Snakes are not aggressive unless provoked. The exception to this is around May or June, when rattlesnakes first come out of hibernation. They are blind, or almost so, and this vulnerability makes them more aggressive than usual. It's a good idea to keep your dog leashed during this time of year and to stay on cleared trails.

The East Bay Regional Parks District has information available about how to react when encountering animals. This is posted at park entrances and in brochures at trailheads.

Small animals, such as rodents and birds, are a significant part of the ecosystem in the parks. They are a part of the food chain, they distribute seeds, and are delight to watch. Respect them by keeping your distance.

Poison Oak: This does exist in most of the parks, and it is important to learn how to identify it so you can avoid it. For most of the year it can be easily recognized by its shiny leaves, three to a stem, with scalloped edges. In winter the leaves drop, and the remaining branches can still release their poison. Don't make the mistake many people have made, thinking you are immune to poison oak. A thorough scrubbing immediately after taking a hike often eliminates any problem. There are also products on the market that can help avoid or minimize problems if you do touch it.

Trails: If a trail is labeled "Road" you can bet that it is an old ranch or carriage road converted into a hiking trail. Many of these trails are wide enough for a vehicle to pass. Narrow trails, also called footpaths (or single track in some guides) are either

9

official park paths or livestock/wildlife trails and will accommodate one or two hikers abreast. Large groups often prefer the roads so that 4 or 5 people can walk side by side. Others prefer the footpaths that tend to wander among trees and less traveled parts of the parks. Read the trail description if this is important to you.

Children: The best way to introduce the little ones to hiking is to have a specific destination in mind. They do best if they know that there is something fun to do when they get there such as climbing, wading in a creek, or swimming. The "Hikes by Attraction" section lists trails meeting these specifications. Read about the hike to decide if it's a good choice for your child. Also, keep in mind the length and altitude gain of the hike, especially for the very young.

Always take along munchies that the kids can put in their pockets, such as cereal or trail mix.

A special word about shoes: The most important thing is fit. Hiking boots aren't always necessary and in some cases might be too heavy for children. Rubber soles with some tread on them are important to prevent slipping in both dry and wet conditions. Good hiking socks, can prevent painful blisters.

Hikes by Attractions

The following list of hikes by attraction will help you find just what you are looking for. The number(s) following each park represent the number of the hike in this book.

Great views:
> Del Valle: Hike 11
> Finley Road: Hike 1
> Las Trampas: Hikes 5, 8, 10, 11
> Los Vaqueros: Hikes 2, 4**
> Morgan Territory: Hikes 7, 8
> Pleasanton Ridge: Hike 7
> Sunol: Hikes 5, 8, 10, 11**, 12**, 13

Shady hikes for hot days (approximately 50% or more of the hike is shade)
> Del Valle: Hike 3
> Finley Road: Hike 2**
> Las Trampas: Hikes 2, 3**, 7, 8, 10
> Macedo Ranch: Hike 1**
> Morgan Territory: Hikes 4**, 6, 10
> Pleasanton Ridge: Hike 1
> Sunol: Hikes 4, 13
> Sycamore Grove: Hike 1**

Good spring wildflowers:
> Del Valle: Hikes 2, 6**, 11
> Las Trampas: Hike 9
> Macedo Ranch: Hikes 1**, 2
> Morgan Territory: Hikes 2, 3, 4**, 8
> Pleasanton Ridge: Hike 7
> Sunol: Hikes 2**, 5, 6, 7**

Good for young children:
      Brushy Peak: Hike 1
      Del Valle: Hike 1
      Las Trampas: Hike 1
      Macedo Ranch: Hike 1**
      Morgan Territory: Hike 1
      Sunol: Hikes 1, 3**
      Sycamore Grove: Hike 1**

Creek or lakeside hiking (a significant portion of the hike):
      Del Valle: Hikes 1, 9**, 10
      Las Trampas: Hikes 1, 2, 3**
      Los Vaqueros: Hike 1
      Macedo Ranch: Hikes 1**, 2
      Morgan Territory: Hikes 3, 4**, 10
      Pleasanton Ridge: Hike 6
      Sunol: Hikes 1, 3**, 4, 7**
      Sycamore Grove: Hike 1

Single Track/footpath hiking (a significant portion of the hike):
      Del Valle: Hikes 2, 4, 6
      Las Trampas: Hikes 3**, 6**, 7
      Macedo Ranch: Hike 3**
      Morgan Territory: Hikes 3, 4
      Pleasanton Ridge: Hikes 1, 2, 4
      Sunol: Hikes 2, 3, 4, 7, 8, 11**

Some Fall color:
      Finley Road: Hikes 1, 2**
      Las Trampas: Hikes 2, 7, 12
      Macedo Ranch: Hikes 1**, 2, 3**
      Morgan Territory: Hikes 1, 6
      Pleasanton Ridge: Hike 5**
      Sunol: Hikes 1, 2, 3, 4, 7, 10, 11, 13

Hikes with some local history:
      Finley Road: Hike 1
      Las Trampas: Hike 3**
      Macedo Ranch: Hike 2
      Morgan Territory: Hike 10
      Pleasanton Ridge: Hike 3
      Sunol: Hikes 6**, 8
      Sycamore Grove: Hike 2

For those short on time but wanting some exercise. These hikes have a good climb early in the hike:
      Del Valle: Hike 5
      Las Trampas: Hikes 2, 5, 8
      Morgan Territory: Hike 3
      Pleasanton Ridge: Hike 2

**Authors' favorite hikes

Brushy Peak Regional Preserve

Overview

Brushy Peak Regional Preserve is a park in the making. Originally limited to the mountain peak itself, East Bay Regional Park District and the Livermore Area Recreation and Park District (LARPD) acquired the land around the peak and are joint caretakers in the Preserve's management and protection. A massive restoration project is in the works to revive the Preserve's seasonal wetlands area, home to the endangered California red-legged frog and the California tiger salamander. Early ranchers left ponds, which are also being restored as part of the wetlands project.

New trails generally follow old ranch roads, as this area is still a working ranch. Expect to see numerous cows and perhaps even a rancher tooling around on an ATV. The trails pass stands of eucalyptus trees, perhaps signs of early homesteads established after the Mexican ranchos became part of the United States. Native Americans roamed, lived and traded on and around Brushy Peak. and have left signs of their occupation, all visible on an escorted pre-scheduled trip with LARPD personnel. This tour is the only way to reach the actual peak, as the preserve's trails stop short of the top.

Beautiful open grassland dominates the terrain; it is mostly non-native grass brought in by ranchers during a couple of hundred years of cultivation. There are a variety of multi-hued wildflowers in spring, especially those that depend on grazing cattle to clear the tall grasses. Summer is not so kind to midday hikers in the Preserve, as there are few trees on most of the trails. Most of the native oak and buckeye trees are located on Brushy Peak, a little too far away to shade the trails. Any time of year, however, is a good time to visit Brushy Peak Regional Preserve, because just a quick climb reveals expansive views of the Livermore Valley.

Brushy Peak Regional Preserve

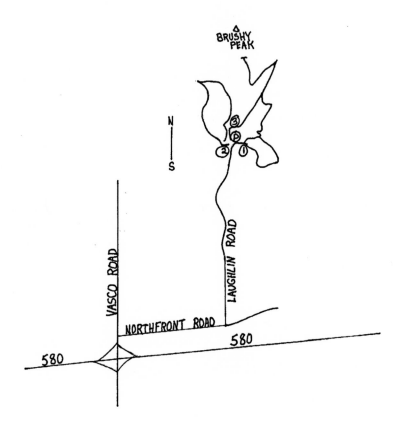

Directions to Laughlin Ranch Staging Area at Brushy Peak Regional Preserve

Note that directions are from the intersection of Highways 580 and 680.

Take 580 east. Take the Vasco Road exit and turn north. Go over the freeway and immediately turn right onto Northfront Road. At the stop sign turn left onto Laughlin Road. Follow this to the end. Park in the Laughlin Ranch Staging Area.

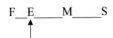
Brushy Peak Regional Preserve: Hike 1
Laughlin Ranch Loop

This trail climbs gradually through the east side of the old Laughlin Ranch. Since the family is still living here, expect to bump into a few cattle along the way. The only trees visible along this hike are far away, so be prepared for lots of sun. The open grassland is, although stark, beautiful in its own way, as it is so typical of California. The lower level of the trail skirts the impressive wetland restoration project, home to native amphibian species, as well as wild birds

Highlights:
❖ Views
❖ Sunny and open
❖ Wetlands

Trail Details:
Distance: 1.9 miles
Time: ¾ hour
Altitude Gain: 370'

Trail Map: East Bay Regional Park District – Brushy Peak

Getting there: Park in the Laughlin Road Staging Area in Brushy Peak Regional Preserve.

The trail: Walk through the gate just beyond the restroom. Laughlin Ranch Loop heads out in a southerly direction and begins to climb towards a clump of eucalyptus trees. It makes two left turns in the next mile and a half before descending and coming to a junction with Tamcan Trail.

Bear left at this junction and continue on Laughlin Ranch Loop back to the parking area. Observe the restoration work in progress as the trail passes next to the wetlands on the right. This is a good spot to stop and look for wildlife, especially with binoculars.

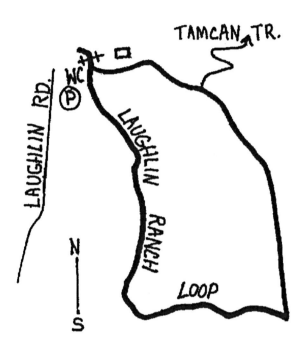

Brushy Peak Regional Preserve: Hike 2
West Side Loop Trail

Don your cowboy hat and head to the hills for the round up, as this is a working ranch as well as a preserve. The trail climbs gradually up the western side of the preserve to just below Brushy Peak. From this point in the trail, a spectacular view of the Livermore Valley is revealed. Then the trail drops steeply into a small valley and passes a spring fed pond. This pond drains water into the wetland restoration area, home of the protected red-legged frogs and California tiger salamanders.

Highlights:
- ❖ View of the valley
- ❖ Wetlands
- ❖ Working ranch
- ❖ Open grassland

Trail Details:
Distance: 2 ¼ miles
Time: 50 minutes
Altitude Gain: 400'

Trail Map: East Bay Regional Park District – Brushy Peak

Getting there: Park in the Brushy Peak parking lot.

The Trail: Walk back to Laughlin Road and go through the gate straight ahead. West Side Loop Trail begins climbing, and continues for about 20 minutes. The view opens up dramatically as the trail peaks. Continue around the small hilltop to the left. The trail makes a sharp right turn at a trail sign and begins a steep descent.

On the left is a large cow pond, constructed by ranchers in the past. It drains into the several acre wetlands restoration area that the trail skirts on the way back. Watch for a variety of wildfowl and an elusive golden eagle. Return through the gate back to the parking area.

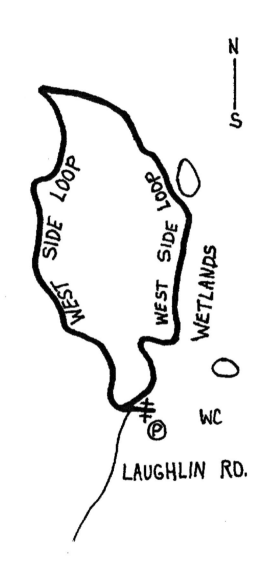

Brushy Peak Regional Park: Hike 3
Brushy Peak Trail

Brushy Peak is in view on this trail but never reached. However, because it gets close to the peak, there is more vegetation than on the other trails in this park. Several small canyons that carry small rivulets into the wetlands area below support a few water-loving trees and bushes.

Because this is still a working ranch, friendly cattle traverse these canyons, trampling many riparian plants that may want to grow here. Even so, it's beautiful open country with expansive views of the Livermore Valley and ranch lands.

Highlights:
❖ Views of Livermore Valley
❖ Large pond with water fowl
❖ Easily shortened
❖ Ranchlands

Trail Details:
Distance: 6.3 miles
Time: 2 ¼ hours
Altitude Gain:1200'

Trail Map: East Bay Regional Park District – Brushy Peak

Getting there: Park in the Laughlin Road Staging Area in Brushy Peak Regional Preserve.

The Trail: To begin this hike walk back to the road and cross it. Continue straight, then shortly bear right onto West Side Loop Trail and follow the wetland preserve north towards Brushy Peak. Pass the large pond, and when the trail begins to climb, take the first branch to the right - a footpath and the beginning of Brushy Peak Loop Trail. This trail climbs over a small hill just below Brushy Peak then descends.

Go through the gate, walk .40 miles. Turn left at the next gate onto Tamcan Trail. After almost a mile, turn left on Laughlin Ranch Loop. This loops to the right back to the parking lot.

Option: To shorten the hike by 1½ miles and eliminate the last climb, stay on Brushy Peak Loop Trail all the way back to the parking area.

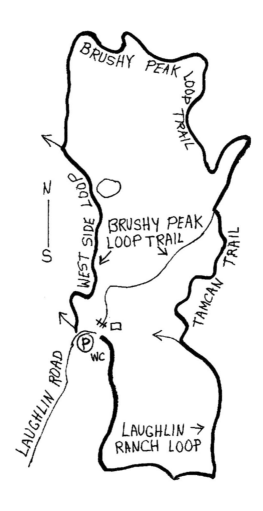

Del Valle Regional Park

Overview

A few minutes south of Livermore a road leads to the crest of a hill and into a typical Northern California landscape of beautiful golden hills, one after another, dotted by oak woodlands and grazing cattle. As the road descends the hill, a glimpse of Livermore's jewel, Lake Del Valle, fills the canyon below. Miles of scenic trails can be found on both sides of the lake and in the hills. One trail that begins in the park links to Del Valle to Sunol Regional Wilderness and then on to Mission Peak via a 28-mile trail through the Ohlone Wilderness.

Two parallel ranges of hills trailing northwest to southeast form the trough that holds the lake water back for approximately five miles. Before the dam was built, this same canyon cradled a natural stream that meandered down to the Cresta Blanca Winery, forming swimming and fishing holes on its way. Many mourn the flooding of this creek but also find it difficult not to find beauty in the new lake. Hiking the scenic seven-mile trail that begins at one end of the lake and finishes at the other end is the best way to see the entire shoreline.

The lake is primarily used for recreation, and swimmers, fishers, boaters and windsurfers find space for their sport. The hills remain for those who prefer to use their feet (and hooves) to survey the countryside and its wildlife. Wonderful habitats surround this lake providing food, water, and shelter for whole communities of animal and plant species. Wildflower fans will be pleased by the variety of flowers from early February in the higher slopes of Rocky Ridge, to early summer in the lower areas.

Del Valle Regional Park

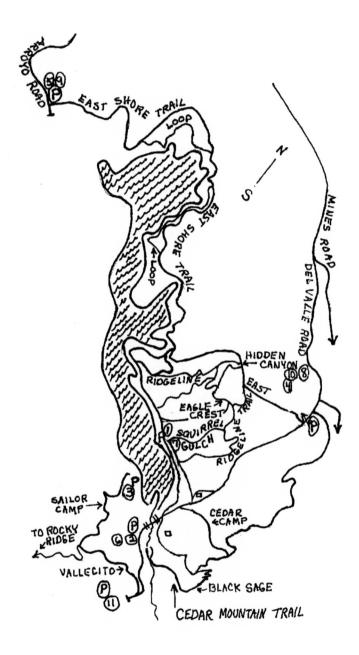

Directions to Del Valle Regional Park

Note that all directions are from the intersection of Highways 580 and 680.

Del Valle main entrance: 580 east. Exit at Vasco Road and turn south. Turn right when Vasco ends at Tesla Road. Go left on Mines Road. After about 3 miles, bear right on Del Valle Road when it splits from Mines Road.

Arroyo Road Staging Area: 580 east. Exit at Portola Ave. Go right on L St. This becomes Arroyo Rd. Follow it to the end.

Del Valle Road parking area: Go toward the main park entrance. Shortly after Mendenhall Road meets Del Valle Road on the left, park in the small unpaved parking area at the top of the hill on the right. This is about ½ mile before the park entrance kiosk.

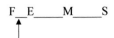

Del Valle Regional Park: Hike 1
East Shore Trail

Lake views dominate this easy trail that meanders along the lake. It is a great place to bird watch, especially early in the day. It is also a designated dog trail. There are restrooms and picnic tables along the way. The basic hike follows the lake out and back, but a short moderate loop can easily be added for a little more exercise and nice overlooks.

Highlights:
- ❖ Constant lake views
- ❖ Length is easily modified
- ❖ Designated dog trail
- ❖ Lake access

Trail Details:
Distance: 2.2 miles
Time: 1 hour
Altitude gain: 80'

Trail Map: East Bay Regional Park District – Del Valle

Getting there: At the main park entrance turn right and park in the farthest lot. The trail starts next to the lake just beyond the boat ramp.

The trail: Follow almost flat East Shore Trail along the lake. Enjoy the serene beauty of the lake, where you might spot a majestic great blue heron or a white egret. After a mile the trail reaches Venados Camp where there are several picnic tables. To return, reverse direction and return to the parking lot.

Option: To add a moderate loop to your hike, at Venados Camp veer right at the fork, go through the gate onto Swallow Bay Trail (also called Venados Trail), and follow the shady trail as it climbs above Badger Cove, offering magnificent lake overlooks. After about 15 minutes, follow the trail to the left as it descends and meets the fire road. This is called Shadow Cliffs to Del Valle Regional Trail. Turn right onto the road, climbing until you reach a "T" intersection. Turn right at the "T" onto Ridgeline and descend back to East Shore Trail. Turn left and follow East

Shore back to the parking lot. With this optional loop, the hike is about 3½ miles, 1½ hours, and has a 400' altitude gain.

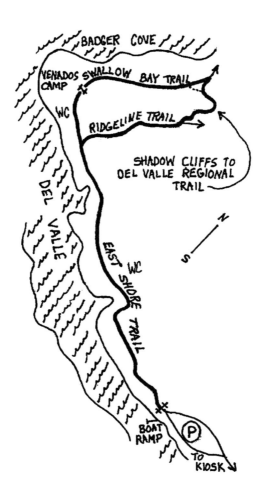

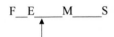
Del Valle Regional Park: Hike 2
Cedar Camp Trail

This is a relatively easy short hike, with some very nice views of the lake as well as beautiful scenery. The main trail can be done in less than an hour, and the ponds and lakeside walking make this a good hike for children. There is also a short, pleasant and very easy optional addition.

Highlights:
- Lake view
- Picnic facilities
- Ponds
- Blue oak grove

Trail Details:
Distance: 2.9 miles
Time: 1 hour
Altitude gain: 450'

Trail Map: East Bay Regional Park District – Del Valle

Getting there: Go to the main park entrance. Continue straight about ½ mile. Cross the bridge and park in the small parking area immediately on the left.

The trail: Walk back over the bridge and turn right on the service road at the end of the bridge. After a few feet, make a sharp hairpin right onto East Shore Trail. The trail goes under the bridge; bear right and follow the lake shore, which isn't always visible because of the brush. After a half-mile, turn right onto an unnamed connector trail that climbs a short distance to the road. Cross the road, walk a few steps to the left and go through the gate on your right. You are now on Cedar Camp Trail.

Follow this narrow trail along a forested canyon wall and it comes to a group picnic area. There are a couple of ponds that mallard ducks call home. The trail turns right and continues to climb a short distance, turns right again, then descends gradually down to the service yard area and on to the bridge. Cross the bridge back to the parking area.

Option: After the first right turn out of Cedar Camp, as you climb the hill there is an optional trail to the right. This short addition is well worth the effort, especially for birdwatchers. It goes near the water treatment ponds (good place for bird watching), and has a nice lake overlook. At the trail's end there is a beautiful grove of blue oak trees - a great spot for a snack. Return back to the main trail. This option adds 1/3 mile to the hike.

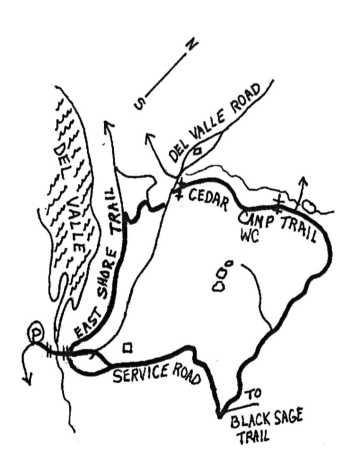

Del Valle Regional Park: Hike 3
Sailor Camp

This is a subset of the Rocky Ridge hike, and a wonderful hike when you want to get away but time is short. It offers lots of morning shade and lush scenery as the trail meanders along a riparian creek. There is enough of an ascent in the first half to get some exercise. It is best not to do this hike right after it rains, as the steep downhill can be very slippery.

Highlights:
- ❖ Variety of native trees
- ❖ Riparian creek
- ❖ Mostly shade
- ❖ Wildflowers and ferns

Trail Details:
Distance: 2.8 miles
Time: 1 ¼ hours
Altitude gain: 550'

Trail Map: East Bay Regional Park District – Del Valle

Getting there: At the main park entrance go straight. Cross the bridge and turn right at the end of the road. Park in the last parking lot on your right.

The trail: Sailor Camp Trail starts from the other side of the road, directly opposite the parking lot. Follow the signs for Ohlone Wilderness Trail. The trail starts climbing steadily right away, and the many oak trees offer some welcome shade on a hot morning.

After approximately 25 minutes you will reach the Sign-in Panel for the Ohlone Trail. Directly opposite the panel to the left is Vallecito Trail; turn left. This is the most beautiful section of the hike as the trail meanders along a riparian creek. It is filled with ferns, a variety of oak, maple and bay trees, and wildflowers beginning in early spring. The steep downhill section of the trail can be quite slippery if muddy or very dry.

The trail continues to descend as it leads to the paved road. When you see signposts to the right of the path, cross the road and enter the campground. Turn left between the kiosk and the store. Follow this road until it comes to Wild Turkey Group Camp. Stay straight and go under the bridge (this is now the West Shore Trail). This follows the lake, and then turns away from the lake back to the parking lot.

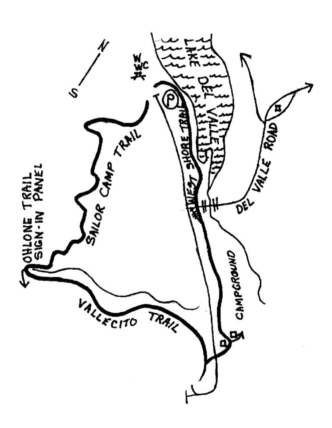

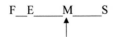

Del Valle Regional Park: Hike 4
Tarantula Cove

Unlike most hikes, this loop starts with a descent to the lake, and ends with a climb back up to the car. Part of the hike is on a narrow unnamed path that follows a downhill contour under shady oaks. The scenery is varied, including beautiful groves of oak trees and the ever-spectacular Lake Del Valle. If time allows, bring your swimsuit and have a quick dip while at the lake.

Highlights:
❖ Views of Lake Del Valle
❖ Shade
❖ Blue oak forest
❖ Lakeside hiking and swimming

Trail Details:
Distance: 4.4 miles
Time: 1¾ hours
Altitude Gain: 650'

Trail Map: East Bay Regional Park District – Del Valle

Getting there: Park at the Del Valle Road parking area prior to the main park entrance.

The trail: Go through the gate to the trailhead for East Ridge Trail. Follow the trail for about 15 minutes. Take a sharp left hairpin turn onto Ridgeline Trail. Follow this trail for 5-10 minutes as it makes a broad right U turn, then bear right onto Eagle Crest (Ridgeline continues to the left). After another 5-10 minutes of descent, the trail meanders off to the right. At this point, bear slightly left onto a narrow footpath (the main trail continues off to the right). If you reach the bottom of the hill, with a seasonal pond on the right, you will need to back up a few yards. Follow the narrow footpath, as it descends gradually to Tarantula Cove and the lake.

Turn right and walk along East Shore Trail just a few minutes to Hetch Hetchy Trail. Look across the lake and try to find the eagles' nest up high in the trees. If you are lucky you might find

34

some birdwatchers with their telescopes focused on the nest; ask them if you can sneak a peak. It's quite a thrill!

Turn right onto Hetch Hetchy Trail. After about 15 minutes make a very sharp right turn onto Ridgeline. Bear left when it intersects with East Ridge Trail and stay on this trail to the parking area.

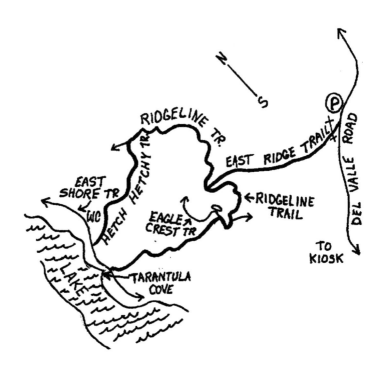

F__E____M____S

Del Valle Regional Park: Hike 5
Arroyo Road/Lake Loop

This trail is a recent addition to the north end of Lake Del Valle. It has a couple of steady climbs on wide gravel trails and also a nice downhill on a narrower trail that heads to the lake and loops back to the main trail. Although there is very little shade on this hike, the lake is almost always in view giving the illusion of coolness. If time is tight, just climb to the top of the hill and return, getting a great cardiovascular workout in less than an hour.

Highlights:
❖ Lake view
❖ Mt. Diablo view
❖ Lake access
❖ Challenging climb

Trail Details:
Distance: 3.9 miles
Time: 1¾ hours
Altitude Gain: 950'

Trail Map: East Bay Regional Park District – Del Valle

Getting there: Park at the Arroyo Road Staging Area.

The trail: Go through the gate and follow the wide trail as it dissects an old walnut orchard. The trail crosses the Arroyo del Valle on a bridge and then comes to another gate. Go through the gate and begin the first of two climbs on this hike. After 20-25 minutes, the trail reaches the top of the hill with the dam on the right. There are two strategically located benches at the top, one overlooking the lake and the other overlooking the valley and Mt. Diablo. Either view is worth the climb.

Take the narrow footpath directly in front of the lake view bench (do not continue down the hill on the main trail). Walk downhill toward the lake, veer left and follow the trail for about ½ mile. The trail climbs gradually back to the main trail. Turn left and continue climbing on the gravel road back to the overlook benches. Return on the same trail to the parking area.

Option: For a shorter version of this hike, climb to the benches at the top of the hill, enjoy the view and return to the parking lot. This totals about 1½ miles, 45 minutes, and an altitude gain of 500'.

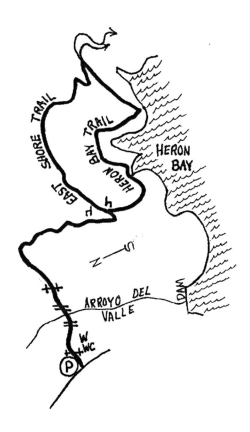

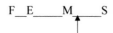
Del Valle Regional Park: Hike 6
Black Sage Trail

This is a good hike if you only have a short time, but would like to enjoy a little nature. The trail crosses a beautiful little creek under a canopy of large shady trees, and wildflowers are abundant in the spring. There are some steep switchbacks midway, but the reward is a picnic table at the top. The trail crosses a larger creek, sometimes not crossable, then it's an easy downhill back to the car.

Highlights:
❖ Spring wildflowers
❖ Summer shade
❖ Hilltop picnic table
❖ Creek crossing

Trail Details:
Distance: 2.7 miles
Time: 1¼ hours
Altitude Gain: 800'

Trail Map: East Bay Regional Park District – Del Valle

Getting there: Go to the main park entrance. Continue straight about ½ mile. Cross the bridge and park in the small parking area immediately on the left.

The trail: (Before beginning this hike, look down from the bridge to see if the creek is passable. If not, turn around at the picnic table and return to the car). Walk back over the bridge and immediately turn right on the service road. Climb about 15 minutes along this road until another road merges in from the left. Pass this road and turn right onto a narrow footpath–a trail marker indicates this is Black Sage Trail. The trail drops down to a gate; pass through the gate and continue. It starts to climb slightly, then meanders down to a stream, crosses the stream and then starts to climb steeply in switchbacks.

About midway into the hike, at the top of the hill there is a picnic table. At this point Black Sage Trail ends and a switchback puts you onto Cedar Mountain Trail that leads down to the larger creek. Look around for a good place to cross. (If there is too much water, retrace your steps instead.) Once across, turn right on the paved campground road. This leads to a restroom on the left and Wild Turkey group camp on the right. Turn right onto the paved trail and after a few hundred feet, climb the stairs on the left up to the parking lot.

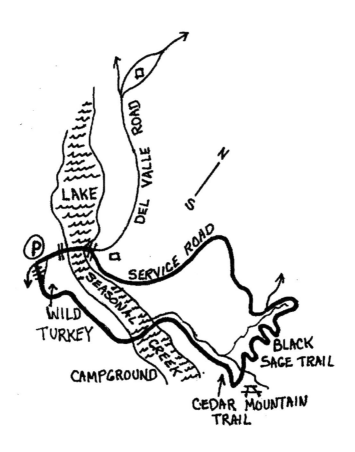

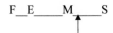

Del Valle Regional Park: Hike 7
Hidden Canyon

Almost half of this hike is along the lake so there is plenty of opportunity to enjoy the acres of blue water. On hot days, don't hesitate to take along bathing gear for a refreshing dip in the lake. The first part of this hike provides all the exercise as the trail ascends from the lake through oak lined canyons so typical of this park. The trail later crosses through open grassland, passing several cow ponds along the way. This hike can be easily shortened by taking one of the many trails down to the lake.

Highlights:
* Lake views
* Oak-lined canyons
* Secluded Trails

Trail Details:
Distance: 5.5 miles
Time: 2 ¼ hours
Altitude Gain: 950'

Trail Map: East Bay Regional Park District – Del Valle

Getting there: At the main park entrance turn right and park in the upper section of the farthest lot. Start at Squirrel Gulch trailhead, across the road by some picnic tables, and through a gate (the sign indicates Fire Trail).

The trail: The hike starts with a short steep climb, followed by some gradual ups and downs. After about 20 minutes turn left onto Ridgeline Trail, following this just a few minutes to Eagle Crest Trail. Turn left and follow Eagle Crest about ¾ mile, then make a sharp hairpin left onto Hidden Canyon Trail. It curves right and passes two trails on the left (to Hetch Hetchy and to Ridgeline). Turn left when it returns to Eagle Crest Trail. After a short climb, go left onto Ridgeline Trail and follow this to a junction.

Stay straight on Ridgeline passing the junctions to Hidden Canyon Trail and Hetch Hetchy Trail. As you travel towards the lake there is a knoll straight ahead, and a trail sign for the

Shadow Cliffs to Del Valle Trail and Hetch Hetchy Trail. Turn right, following the Shadow Cliffs to Del Valle Trail.

Continue following the trail almost to the water's edge. At the next signpost for Shadow Cliffs to Del Valle Trail, turn left. This is called Swallow Bay Trail and overlooks Badger Cove. At the end, go through the gate, turn left onto East Shore Trail and follow it along the lake to the parking lot.

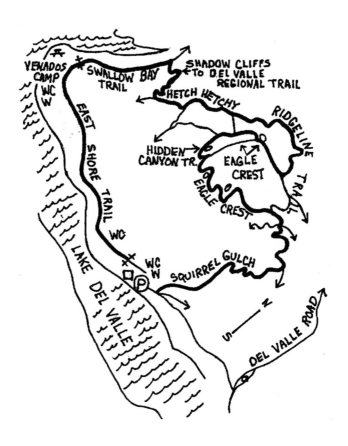

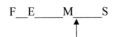

Del Valle Regional Park: Hike 8
East Side/West Side Loop

This trail explores one of the newest sections of the park. It begins downhill, drops down almost to the lake and then climbs back to the starting point. The downhill part of the hike travels through an old ranch that the park still leases out for grazing. Watch for many wildflowers in these open fields in the spring. At the midpoint, the trail passes close to the lake, a good place to break and watch the shorebirds in winter when the lake is low.

Highlights:
- ❖ Long downhill with view
- ❖ Shoreline habitat
- ❖ Wildflowers

Trail Details:
Distance: 6.2 miles
Time: 2½ hours
Altitude Gain: 950'

Trail Map: East Bay Regional Park District – Del Valle

Getting there: Park at the Del Valle Road parking area prior to the main park entrance. Cross the road and walk back up the road a few yards. There is an entrance gate to the trail.

The trail: Go through the gate and turn right. The trail curves left around the hill and begins descending into the east side of the park. It eventually passes a park ranger's residence and ends at the canyon floor where it intersects with Cedar Camp Trail. Turn right and walk through the group picnic area. The trail continues at the end of the picnic area and narrows to a footpath. Then it climbs slightly along a seasonal creek until it comes to Del Valle Road.

Cross the road, walk a little to the left and look for the narrow trail. It merges with East Shore Trail. Turn right and follow it to the lake. Stop and enjoy the view of the boats and birds. Continue on the path until it approaches a parking lot.

Go through the parking lot, go over the bridge, cross the road, walk a few hundred feet and turn right onto Ridgeline Trail.

Stay left at the trail sign for Lake View Trail and take the far left trail at the next sign. Many trails intersect with Ridgeline so be careful not to get on the wrong trail. Ridgeline twists and turn its way up the hill to East Ridge Trail. Turn right on East Ridge and follow it for 3/4-mile back to the parking area.

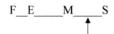

F__E____M____S

Del Valle Regional Park: Hike 9
East Ridge to Dam

This is a wonderful one-way car caravan hike. Start by descending from the top of Del Valle Road toward the lake, and then follow the lake all the way to the dam. The views are magnificent, and the trails offer a good blend of downhill, flat and uphill. Most of the trails follow old ranch roads lined with a variety of native oaks and dotted with grazing cattle. This bucolic landscape is punctuated with lake views and large bays. This trail can be hiked from either direction, but this way keeps the sun at your back until afternoon.

Highlights:
❖ Lakeside hiking
❖ Long but not strenuous
❖ Balance of hills and flats
❖ Long downhill start

Trail Details:
Distance: 7 miles
Time: 3 hours
Altitude gain: 950'

Trail Map: East Bay Regional Park District – Del Valle

Getting there: Leave one car at the Arroyo Road Staging Area. Take a second car to the Del Valle Road parking area.

The trail: The hike starts on East Ridge Trail and descends steadily downhill for about an hour. After 15 minutes, East Ridge Trail merges into Ridgeline Trail; continue straight. Ridgeline turns right and passes Eagle Crest Trail. Turn right when the trail comes to a T at Hetch Hetchy Trail.

After 1/3 mile turn right where a signpost says 'Shallow Cliffs to Del Valle Regional Trail'. Stay on this trail as it approaches Badger Cove. Bear right and follow East Shore Trail all the way to Heron Bay, toward the dam. Note that some signposts are marked 'East Shore' and others 'Del Valle to Shadow Cliffs'; these are the same trail.

44

At the top of the last hill are two benches, one overlooking Heron Bay, the other facing the Livermore Valley and Mount Diablo. This is a breathtaking view and a welcome rest spot! From here it's about a 15-minute descent to the parking lot; be sure to take in the view of the Wente Golf Course in the foreground - a stunning patch of green against the golden summertime hills.

F_E____M___S

Del Valle Regional Park: Hike 10
Arroyo Road/Heron Bay Loop

This fairly steep trail is a great way to see the northwest end of Lake Del Valle. The trail leads through an old orchard, crosses a year-round creek, and climbs 500' to a stupendous view of the end of the lake and the Livermore Valley. A small loop trail leads down to the edge of the lake, and back to the main trail. In the summer, do this hike early in the day, as there is little shade.

Highlights:
- ❖ Superb lake and valley views
- ❖ Length of hike easily modified
- ❖ Creek and pond for dogs

Trail Details:
Distance: 7 miles
Time: 3 hours
Altitude Gain:1500'

Trail Map: East Bay Regional Park District – Del Valle

Getting there: Park at the Arroyo Road Staging Area.

The trail: The trail starts at the parking lot and is almost flat as you cross a bridge over the Arroyo del Valle (great for dogs). Then it starts to climb. There is a year-round pond on the left, another favorite dog spot!

After about 20-25 minutes, and a 500 foot climb, you will reach the top. Relax on one of the strategically located benches and enjoy the breathtaking views of Lake Del Valle, Mt. Diablo and the Livermore Valley.

Continue on the main trail as it descends. There is a lower, almost parallel trail called Heron Bay Trail that has several access points and signposts. The first signpost says 'To Dam'. Pass this and three more signposts named 'Heron Bay' as the trail circles Heron Bay. The main trail begins to climb through oak trees to another signpost at the foot of a knoll; this also says 'Heron Bay'. Turn right. The trail drops to Heron Bay, descending almost to lake level, then curves around one of the bay's larger inlets.

Heron Bay Trail starts to ascend again and loops back to the main trail at the fourth signpost. Turn left and follow it back to the bench at the top of the hill and then return to the parking lot. For more lakeside hiking on narrow footpaths, take any of the small loop trails to the left of the main trail. These all lead back to the bench at the top of the hill, crisscrossing the main trail now and then.

Note that in some places main trail is called "East Shore", and others "Del Valle to Shadow Cliffs."

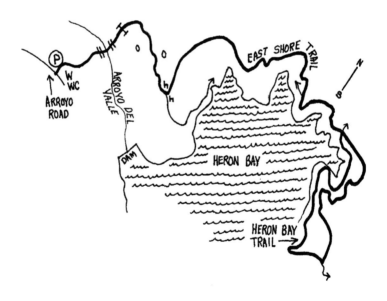

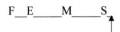

Del Valle Regional Park: Hike 11
Rocky Ridge

You will love this hike if you like good steep continuous climbing and spectacular views. The trail starts out along a beautiful shady cascading creek with overgrown ferns and shade-loving wildflowers in season. The first half of the trail is all uphill making this a good workout hike. But be careful of your footing going down if the trail is muddy or very dry.

Highlights:
- ❖ 360 degree views
- ❖ Great aerobic workout
- ❖ Spring wildflowers on top
- ❖ Lush shaded creek

Trail Details:
Distance: 4.5 miles
Time: 2 ½ hours
Altitude Gain:1750'

Trail Map: East Bay Regional Park District – Del Valle

Getting there: At the main park entrance, stay left. Cross the bridge and turn left. Go to the end of the road, onto the gravel. Park in the equestrian area on the right

Permit Required: A permit is required for use of the Ohlone Wilderness Trail. Contact park headquarters for information.

The trail: The trail starts as Vallecito Trail. After a level beginning, it climbs for about ¾ mile, following a riparian creek. At the Ohlone Trail Sign-in Panel, turn left onto the Ohlone Trail and continue for about a mile.

Turn right at heavily shaded Stromer Spring identified by a cattle trough and a well pump. Continue climbing to Rocky Ridge, turn left and continue walking along top of the ridge, absorbing the beautiful views of Mount Diablo and the Livermore Valley. Also note the variety of spring wildflowers and the colorful lichen on the large boulders. Continue straight on Rocky Ridge and go left on the Ohlone Trail to complete a loop. Pass the Stromer Spring turnoff and bear right. When you get back to the Sign-in Panel, turn right onto Vallecito Trail, which goes back to the trailhead.

Option: At the top, continue right on the Ohlone Trail, descend steeply to Williams Gulch, a heavily shaded creek. This adds about 1½ miles round trip to the hike. Just be sure to reserve some energy for the steep hike back up to Rocky Ridge.

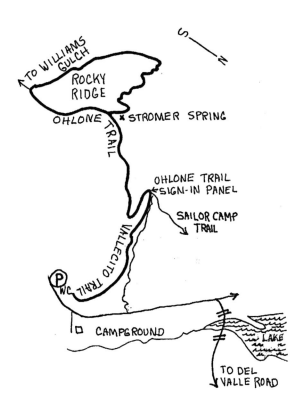

Finley Road
Access to Western Morgan Territory
and Mt. Diablo State Park

Overview

This spectacular wilderness area is nestled at the southern foot of Mt. Diablo, in the backcountry of the Tri-Valley between Livermore, Dublin and San Ramon; it includes the western-most section of Morgan Territory Regional Preserve. This is a much less known part of the park and the access is so far from the other areas of Morgan Territory, that it is worthy of its own section in this book.

Finley Road, a two lane country road, leads to the trailhead called Old Finley Road. A half-mile from the entrance, a slight widening in the road provides the closest parking spot. The one half mile walk is worth the effort, though, as this area is not only spectacular in itself, but also connects to miles and miles of trails in Mt. Diablo State Park and Morgan Territory.

There is some history to this area, as Old Finley Road has existed in its present state for a hundred years or so. Wagons used the road to get to Morgan Territory Road, and you can still get there on the same road, though only on foot! Since it was once used for travel, Old Finley Road is fairly level for about a mile. Old ranch roads lead away from this main trail into the hills and deep wooded canyons, and now provide good walking trails. This is one of the least used wilderness in the East Bay Parks, so it is teeming with wildlife, wildflowers, and birds, although often elusive. Some remnants of old ranch buildings and fences still dot the landscape, as well as resident cattle from surviving ranching enterprises.

Riggs Canyon Trail and Oyster Point Trail in Mount Diablo State Park can be reached by a trail beginning right after an old ranch house, only a short walk from the Old Finley Road trailhead. Highland Ridge Trail also extends deep into Morgan Territory, providing additional miles of backcountry hiking.

Finley Road Access to Western Morgan Territory and Mt. Diablo State Park

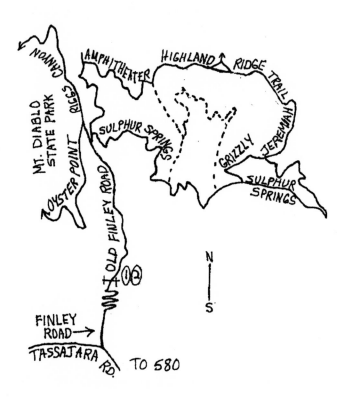

Directions To Finley Road

Note that directions are from the intersection of Highways 580 and 680.

Take Highway 580 east. Exit at Tassajara/Santa Rita. Turn north on Tassajara. Follow this about 3½ miles, then turn right onto Finley Road and continue to the end. Backtrack about ½ mile to a shoulder on the left side of the street and park under a cluster of large trees.

Finley Road – Hike 1
Jeremiah Trail

This challenging trail provides a good sampling of the varied landscape in the northern California hills. It roller-coasters up and down on old roads, narrow footpaths, and cow paths that barely leave an impression in the tall grass. Whatever the footing, the trail leads across open grassland, wooded hills, and dips into deep ravines embedded with the creeks that created them. Beautiful stands of live and blue oaks weave among the canyons, and sycamores shade the creek bottoms.

Highlights:
- Varied landscape
- Views of Mt. Diablo
- Historical road

Trail Details:
Distance: 8.4 miles
Time: 4 ¼ hours
Altitude Gain:1650'

Trail Map: East Bay Regional Park District – Morgan Territory

Getting there: Park in the Finley Road parking area.

The trail: The trail begins about one half mile from the parking area. It follows the old Finley Road, passing right through a couple of ranches at the outset. Continue on this dirt road, meandering under the shade of Bay and Oak trees with a seasonal creek down an escarpment on the right.

Soon after leaving the shade, there is an old house on the left. Continue on the road about a quarter of a mile. On the right is a trail marker for Sulphur Spring Trail. Take this trail and zigzag uphill. After fifteen minutes, the trail flattens out and then winds its way down to Sulphur Spring, providing much shade along the way. A strong sulfur smell will let you know that you have arrived!

A steep climb away from the creek takes you to Grizzly Trail. Turn left and continue climbing until Grizzly Trail ends at Jeremiah Trail. Go straight on Jeremiah until it ends at Highland Ridge Trail, the highest point in this hike. Turn left and enjoy the view of the San Ramon Valley and Mt. Diablo State Park while walking on the ridge. The next trail marker is for Morgan Ridge Trail. Go past this to the next intersection. Where Highland Ridge goes to the right, instead bear left on Crestview. Take the next right turn onto Amphitheater Trail. This is now a fairly shady downhill trek that returns to Finley Road. Turn left and retrace your steps back to the trailhead.

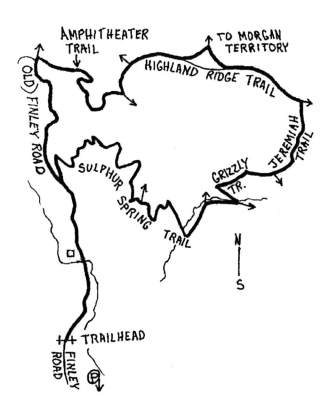

Finley Road: Hike 2
Sulphur Spring Loop

This is a strenuous hike that provides plenty of shade on a hot valley day. After a short sunny climb, the trail goes under the cover of substantial California native trees for a couple of miles and skirts a deep and heavily shaded stream bed before climbing out into open grassland. This is a lightly used loop trail sure to please those who want to get away from civilization.

Highlights:
- ❖ Shade
- ❖ Native trees
- ❖ Deep ravine
- ❖ Creek

Trail Details:
Distance: 9.0 miles   5
Time: 4½ hours
Altitude Gain: 1700'

Trail Map: East Bay Regional Park District – Morgan Territory

Getting there: Park in the Finley Road parking area.

The trail: Continue east on Finley Road ½ mile from the parking area and go through the park gate. Keep going straight until the trail changes to a dirt road and becomes very shady. There is a ravine on the right with a seasonal creek. This is the old Finley Road of the horse and buggy era, that connects to Morgan Territory Road.

After leaving the shade there is an old boarded up farmhouse on the left. Continue walking for about ¼ mile and turn right onto Sulphur Spring Trail. Stay on this trail until it crosses Sulphur Creek. Continue, always bearing right passing trails on the left. Sulphur Spring Trail then skirts a ravine on the left shaded with oak and bay trees and a few big leaf maples. The trail makes a sharp hairpin turn left and changes to Jeremiah Trail, climbing up into open country. Turn left on Grizzly Trail and follow it to its end at Sulphur Spring Trail. You have just finished a beautiful loop.

Bear right on Sulphur Spring Trail, retracing your steps to Finley Road. Turn left and return to the trailhead.

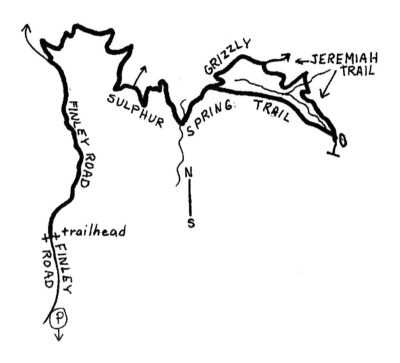

Las Trampas Regional Wilderness

Overview

Las Trampas deserves the title "wilderness", and yet it is so close to the urban East Bay hustle-bustle. In fact, from the busy highway 680, it is only a 10-minute drive to the heart of the park. East Bay Regional Park District has been so careful to preserve the natural setting of this park that even the drive in on Bollinger Canyon Road is a rural experience; your eyes are not fooling you if you see zebras and ostriches along the way. There are about 4,000 acres to tramp around in within the park, and even more as the park connects to the huge East Bay Municipal Utility District. With an EBMUD permit, it is possible to hike from Las Trampas in San Ramon to Moraga and Castro Valley.

The park itself allows for all day hiking in a great variety of terrain. Two ridges, Rocky Ridge and Las Trampas Ridge, run the length of the park with a canyon nestled between them. This canyon is the staging area for most of the hikes in the park. Other staging areas are on the eastern side of Las Trampas Ridge in

Danville. Other than a short hike on the canyon floor, all of the hikes climb one of the two ridges and branch from there. From these ridges there are extensive views of the Carquinez Strait, Mt. Diablo, and the surrounding valleys.

A special feature of Las Trampas is the variation in vegetation zones. On the eastern side of the Las Trampas Ridge, native oak, madrone and buckeye trees heavily dominate the terrain, whereas the eastern side of Rocky Ridge is principally open grassland. The western side of both ridges is covered in a variety of native chaparral such as chamise, black sage and buck brush, as it is more arid than the east side. Deep canyons are shaded with overlapping canopies of bay, big leaf maple and even creek dogwood, perfect for summer hiking.

There are some very challenging trails at Las Trampas but most of them fall into the intermediate category. Many of these have good destination spots such as Las Trampas Peak, Eagle Peak, wind caves, and deep shady canyons. In spring, tall grasses, colorful wildflowers, and babbling creeks fill the canyons, fields, and hills.

Las Trampas Regional Wilderness

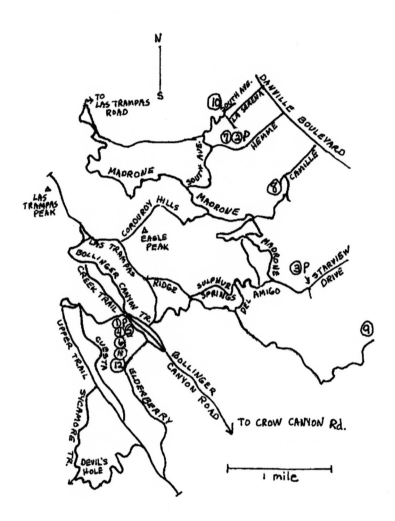

Directions to Las Trampas Regional Wilderness

Note that all directions are from the intersection of Highways 580 and 680.

Main parking lot on Bollinger Canyon Road: Go north on Highway 680. Exit at Crow Canyon and cross over the freeway. Turn right onto Bollinger Canyon Rd. Follow this until it ends, with the park entrance on the left.

Ringtail Cat Staging Area: Go north on Highway 680. Exit at El Cerro. Cross under freeway. Turn right onto Danville Blvd, then left onto Hemme Ave. Continue to the end.

South Ave. street parking: Go north on Highway 680. Exit at El Cerro. Cross under freeway. Turn right onto Danville Blvd, then left onto La Serena. Go right on Holiday Dr, then left on South Ave. Park at the end of South Ave.

Starview Drive street parking: Go north on Highway 680. Exit at El Cerro. Cross under freeway. Turn right onto Danville Blvd. Take the first left on Del Amigo Road. Take the 4th right, the continuation of Del Amigo Road. Take the first left (still Del Amigo). It bears left, then bear right onto Starview Drive. Park on the right.

Remington Loop street parking: From Highway 680 North, take the Sycamore Valley Road exit, cross over the freeway and continue for a half-mile. The street name changes to Remington Drive, then to Remington Loop. Park along the street.

Camille Ave. street parking: Take 680 to the El Cerro exit. Cross under the freeway. Turn right on Danville Boulevard. At Camille, turn left, continue about four blocks, and park on the side of the road just before it turns left.

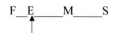
Las Trampas Regional Wilderness: Hike 1
Bollinger Creek Loop Trail

This short trail is special because much of it is along a seasonal creek with a lush overstory of native Bay and Oak trees. In the winter and spring, the creek runs steadily and the trail is right next to it. There is a short climb at the beginning and at the end, so this trail is good for novices just beginning to hike.

Highlights: **Trail Details:**
❖ Creek   Distance: 2.2 miles
❖ Two loops: easily shortened   Time: 1 hour
❖ Mature Bay and Oak trees   Altitude Gain: 350'

Trail Map: East Bay Regional Park District – Las Trampas

Getting there: Park in the main Las Trampas parking lot.

The trail: Go over the bridge at the north end of the parking lot, then turn left onto Bollinger Creek Loop Trail. Follow the trail as it climbs slightly for almost a mile. Watch for a trail marker on the left for Bollinger Creek Loop Trail. Turn left onto this narrow path as it doubles back and begins to follow the creek. About halfway along this trail it splits. Both trails lead back to the bridge, but stay left to follow the creek. This area is entirely shaded with huge California Bay and Oak trees.

The hike can end at the parking lot if time is short. Otherwise, cross over the bridge again, cross the road, turn right and continue on Bollinger Creek Loop Trail. This trail is fairly level as it parallels the road. It will eventually come to a fenced parking area and turn left following the fence. It dips under the trees straight ahead, crosses the small creek bed and continues on the other side.

The trail now leads to the road. Cross the road, walk a few steps to the left, and turn right into the driveway. Go through the gate with a sign for Elderberry Trail. Stay on Elderberry Trail, bear right and continue to the parking area. There is a slight climb on this last segment of the trail, as it leads away from the creek.

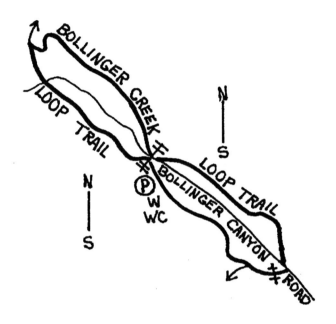

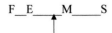

Las Trampas Regional Wilderness: Hike 2
Ringtail Cat Trail

Hot summer days won't interfere with hiking on this mostly shaded trail. A short steady climb at the beginning provides a cardiovascular workout while you enjoy the pretty scenery. Following rainfall, both access trails provide soothing creek sounds and lush vegetation.

Highlights: **Trail Details:**
❖ Mostly shade   Distance: 4.2 miles
❖ View of Mt. Diablo   Time: 1½ hours
❖ Creek   Altitude Gain: 600'

Trail Map: East Bay Regional Park District – Las Trampas

Getting there: Park in the Ringtail Cat Staging Area.

The trail: Ringtail Cat trail leaves from the staging area and meanders along a small creek for a short distance. It then turns left and begins climbing under the shade of native oak trees.

When the trail begins to level, watch for a trail marker for Ringtail Cat/To Madrone Trail. Just before the sign, instead of continuing straight towards Madrone, turn right onto an unnamed footpath. Follow this nicely shaded trail for about a mile as it parallels Madrone, and continue to bear right until it intersects with Madrone Trail near the horse trough.

Turn left onto Madrone, a wide ranch road, and follow it down to the sign for Ringtail Cat Trail. Turn left and continue until it meets the creek. Turn right and return to the parking lot.

This is the shady version of this hike. If you prefer to stay on marked trails, continue past the Ringtail Cat/To Madrone Trail sign as you climb Ringtail Cat Trail, turn right onto Madrone Trail and walk as far as you like before turning around.

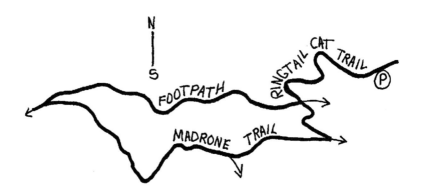

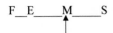
Las Trampas Regional Wilderness: Hike 3
Del Amigo Trail

This shady trail is on the top of the list for a hot summer day when many hikes would be out of the question. After a short initial climb, the trail dips gently up and down, barely leaving the cool cover of native oaks and bay trees. There are a couple of creek crossings that are quite beautiful even in the summer without water. At the end of the hike, the trail wanders through the pasture of the historical Eugene O'Neill homestead.

Highlights:
❖ Mostly shaded
❖ Creek crossings
❖ Historic buildings

Trail Details:
Distance: 3.4 miles
Time: 1¾ hours
Altitude Gain: 950'

Trail Map: East Bay Regional Park District – Las Trampas

Getting there: Follow directions to Starview Drive street parking. The trailhead entrance is through a gate in a chain link fence on the right side of the road where Starview Drive becomes Starmont Court

The trail: Go through the gate in the chain link fence and begin climbing up Del Amigo Trail. After ten minutes, watch for a signpost on the right for Virgil Williams Trail. It can be hard to see, especially when the grass is tall. Turn right and enjoy the shade as the trail dips slightly towards Madrone Trail. Pass through a gate and turn left on Madrone. The shade is deeper here, as the spring-fed trees grow tall with a dense over story of leaves. Madrone turns sharply to the right and reverses direction.

Begin to watch for the signpost for Virgil Williams Trail, which is a narrow footpath off to the right. It descends to a creek bed with beautiful moss covered boulders, a good resting place. Continue on Virgil Williams Trail until it crosses a small footbridge. Turn left onto Madrone Trail. It follows a fence

66

enclosing the Eugene O'Neill homestead, then crosses a pasture and meets with Del Amigo Trail on the other side. Turn left and return to the starting point.

Option: On a hot day, it is shadier to return on Virgil Williams; instead of turning left on Madrone Trail toward the homestead, stay on Virgil Williams. Turn left on Del Amigo and follow it to the trailhead.

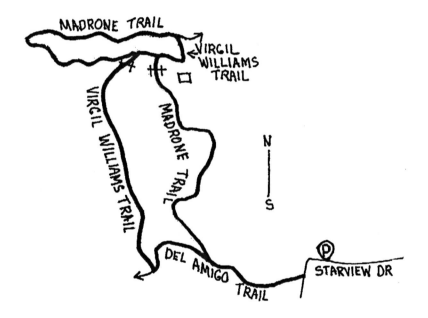

Las Trampas Regional Wilderness: Hike 4
Las Trampas Peak Trail

The top of Las Trampas provides an astounding 360 degree view of the bay area from San Francisco bay to Suisun Bay to Mt. Diablo and points in between! It's not a hike for a hot day, however, as there is very little shade on the return. So save this for a clear winter day when the view is even more spectacular.

Highlights:
❖ 360 degree panoramic views
❖ Madrone trees
❖ Varied vegetation

Trail Details:
Distance: 4 miles
Time: 2 hours
Altitude Gain: 1100'

Trail Map: East Bay Regional Park District – Las Trampas

Getting there: Park in the main Las Trampas parking lot.

The trail: Go over the bridge at the north end of the parking lot, cross the road, walk a short distance, then turn left onto Bollinger Creek Loop Trail. Follow it as it climbs slowly and comes to a saddle. The trail turns right and eventually meets Las Trampas Ridge Trail. Turn left and stay on this all the way to Las Trampas Peak. A small footpath leads to the top of the peak.

Return to Las Trampas Ridge Trail and retrace your steps. After a half mile, the trail continues straight but is hard to see as it narrows and leads through overgrown brush. Just be careful not to bear right onto Bollinger Creek Loop Trail.

The trail is now alternately shady and sunny and passes some magnificent madrone trees. At the fork, turn right onto Chamise Trail and descend to Bollinger Creek Loop Trail. Turn right and after a few minutes turn left and cross the road and bridge to the parking area.

Option: For a recommended side trip to Eagle Peak, turn left onto Corduroy Hills Trail off Las Trampas Ridge Trail and step over the low wooden barrier. The trail crosses a saddle and then scrambles up a rocky trail to the peak, where a bench awaits. Relax and enjoy the view of Mt. Diablo. Return to Las Trampas Ridge Trail. This option adds less than ½ mile and about 200 feet elevation gain.

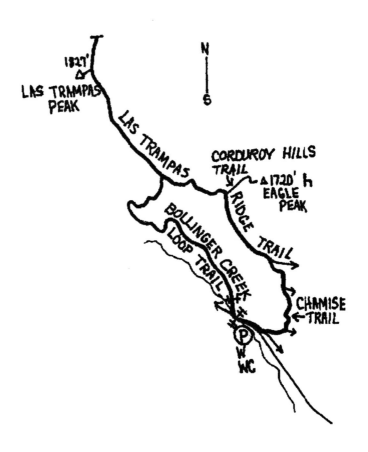

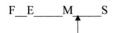
Las Trampas Regional Wilderness: Hike 5
Rocky Ridge View Trail

This loop hike climbs up to Rocky Ridge and then continues fairly level for a mile and a half. Take this time to enjoy the views of the canyon below. Mount Diablo provides a massive backdrop for the view of Las Trampas Ridge to the east. You can optionally add a half-mile by taking Sycamore Trail to see the wind caves in the valley to the west.

Highlights:
- Vast views
- Good cardiovascular workout
- Nice side trip with rock outcroppings

Trail Details:
Distance: 4.6 miles
Time: 2 hours
Altitude Gain: 1150'

Trail Map: East Bay Regional Park District – Las Trampas

Getting there: Park in the main Las Trampas parking lot.

The trail: Walk to the south end of the parking lot and go through the gate onto Elderberry Trail. Stay on this trail for two miles until it reaches Rocky Ridge View Trail. This is mostly uphill, and your cardiovascular workout is done when you reach the top. Turn right on Rocky Ridge View Trail and enjoy the ridge-top walk with panoramic views on both sides. Turn right on Cuesta Trail; a shortcut to Rocky Ridge View Trail. It's a narrow trail with lots of welcome vegetation after the barren terrain. Turn right on Rocky Ridge View Trail and follow it downhill to the parking area.

Option: For a little side trip to a beautiful valley, instead of turning on Cuesta Trail, continue a third mile on Rocky Ridge View Trail and turn left onto Sycamore Trail. This is one mile from the intersection of Rocky Ridge View Trail and Elderberry Trail. Walk down to the rock outcroppings with unusual wind cave formations. Stay on the trail as this is a sensitive ecological area. Return to Rocky Ridge View Trail, turn right, and then left on Cuesta Trail. This option adds an additional 150' altitude gain.

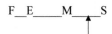

Las Trampas Regional Wilderness: Hike 6
Oak Circle Trail

This hike is a mini journey into the various Northern California ecosystems. To see this variety in one park, on one hike, on one day, is hard to imagine. If followed to its end, this short but strenuous hike will pass through a deep fern laden canyon, dry chaparral hillsides, rocky peaks, open grassland savannas, and shady oak and bay forests. Not to be missed!

Highlights:
- ❖ Great views
- ❖ Deep canyon
- ❖ Native vegetation
- ❖ Aerobic
- ❖ Topographic variety

Trail Details:
Distance: 3.6 miles
Time: 1¾ hours
Altitude Gain: 1400'

Trail Map: East Bay Regional Park District – Las Trampas

Getting there: Park in the main Las Trampas parking lot.

The trail: Go over the bridge at the north end of the parking lot, cross the road, walk a short distance, then turn right onto Bollinger Creek Loop Trail. Turn left on Chamise Trail and then right on Trapline Trail. Stay on this narrow trail, as it descends into a beautiful dense bay tree forest. At the bottom of the canyon, cross a footbridge and bear right, staying on Trapline Trail. The trail now climbs steeply and leads out of the shade cover to a ridge with exceptional views of open grassland, oaks and green (or gold) hills. After almost a half mile, the trail intersects Las Trampas Ridge Trail. Cross this and go straight onto Sulphur Springs Trail. It descends and meets Del Amigo Trail. Turn right.

Del Amigo climbs back to the Las Trampas Ridge Trail. Turn right and enjoy the easy walk along the top of the ridge with views of Mt. Diablo on the right and Rocky Ridge on the left.

Almost a mile later, turn left on Chamise Trail, as it meanders through typical California chaparral. Shortly, turn left on Mahogany Trail, descending again into the bay forest filled canyon. At the bottom, turn right on Trapline and climb out to meet Chamise Trail. Turn left and descend to Bollinger Creek Loop Trail. Turn right and return to the parking area.

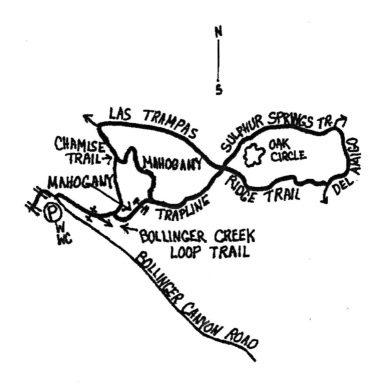

Las Trampas Regional Wilderness: Hike 7
Las Trampas Road

There is abundant shade on this trail as it hugs canyon walls forested with California Bay and Oak trees. The trail climbs sharply for 500 feet and then more gradually until the end where it drops steeply as it snakes along a canyon ridge. Along the way, there are spectacular views of Mt. Diablo and the Sacramento River. Watch for the red barked Madrone trees that are larger here than in any other of the Tri-Valley parks. Many creeks intersect the trail in winter but are easy to cross. Be careful of your footing on the descent if the trail is muddy or very dry.

Highlights:
❖ Lots of shade
❖ Big Leaf Maple forest
❖ Fall color
❖ Huge Madrone trees
❖ Winter creek crossings

Trail Details:
Distance: 4.9 miles
Time: 2 ½ hours
Altitude Gain: 1350'

Trail Map: East Bay Regional Park District – Las Trampas

Getting there: Park in the Ringtail Cat Staging Area.

The trail: Go through the open gate from the staging area and follow Ringtail Cat Trail along the creek until it meets South Avenue Trail. Turn left, and begin the ascent to Madrone Trail. Turn right onto Madrone, and leave the trees for a short time as the trail comes out into the open. Or for more shade, take the footpath described in Ringtail Cat Trail hike.

The trail bears right and becomes shaded with California Bay trees. When the trail comes to a trail marker for trail marker and says "to Las Trampas Peak". Madrone Trail also turns left here but stay straight.

In approximately a half-hour a gate crosses the trail. Turn right onto a footpath just before the gate instead of going through it. This trail becomes heavily shaded and loops back to almost touch the trail you walked on earlier. Watch carefully now as the trail can disappear for a few feet, especially in winter. Stay straight as it begins a fairly steep and rapid descent to South Avenue trail, traveling along a roller coaster ridge top the entire way. At the end of the last descent, turn right at the intersection with South Avenue trail. Cross the creek, turn left at the "Y" onto Ringtail Cat Trail and return to the staging area.

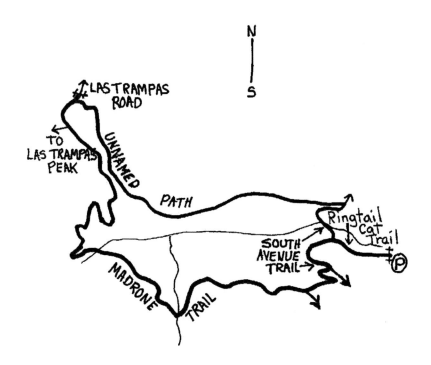

Las Trampas Regional Park: Hike 8
Camille Trail

This is a simple hike to follow, but it isn't simple to climb! Fortunately, native oak and California bay trees provide good shade cover for over half of this hike. The first half of the hike is uphill, so the shade is very welcome in summer. As if that isn't enough, spectacular high altitude views of Mt. Diablo are visible after the first mile of this hike and all the way down.

Highlights:
- ❖ Great workout
- ❖ Vast views
- ❖ Lots of shade

Trail Details:
Distance: 4.9 miles
Time: 2 ¾ hours
Altitude Gain: 1600'

Trail Map: East Bay Regional Park District – Las Trampas

Getting there: Follow directions to the Camille Ave. street parking.

The trail: The trailhead is located on the west side of Camille Ave., just as the street turns left. The trail is fenced in on both sides for the first two blocks and is next to an orchard. At the end of the fenced-in area, the trail begins to climb through an old eucalyptus grove, then comes out into the open under some scattered oak trees. Pass the first junction to the left and continue for almost a mile to the junction with Corduroy Trail. Veer left onto Corduroy Trail and continue climbing.

The trail narrows as it nears Eagle Peak and is quite shady. At the top, stay left and continue to the peak. A bench is there for a much-deserved rest. The view of Mt. Diablo is outstanding.

Continue to enjoy this view on the downhill walk, retracing the same trails on Corduroy, then Madrone, and back to Camille Avenue.

76

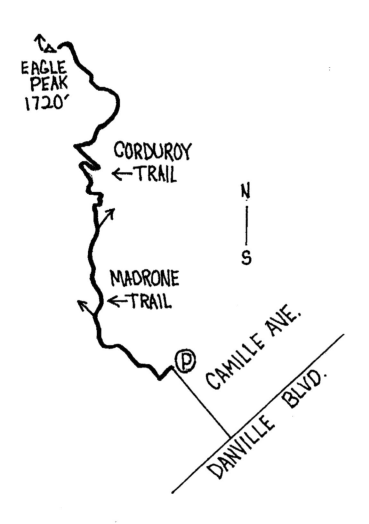

EAGLE
PEAK
1720'

CORDUROY
←TRAIL

N
|
S

MADRONE
←TRAIL

P CAMILLE AVE.

DANVILLE BLVD.

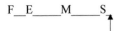
Las Trampas Regional Park: Hike 9
Remington Road Trail

Non stop views dominate this hike as it meanders through wide-open grassy terrain to Las Trampas Ridge. It is a special spring hike among tall green fields of grass and an abundance of wildflowers. The trail skirts around Oak Circle at the high point in this hike, descending on a shady path to a seasonal creek, and then up to the ridge again. There is a lot of climbing on this hike, but it is gradual so less noticed than more strenuous hikes.

Highlights:
❖ Aerobic
❖ Spectacular open views
❖ Abundant spring wildflowers

Trail Details:
Distance: 7.1 miles
Time: 3 hours
Altitude Gain: 2000'

Trail Map: East Bay Regional Park District – Las Trampas

Getting there: Follow directions to Remington Loop street parking. Watch for the trailhead on the right. It is at a brown metal gate after 246 Remington Loop.

The trail: Enter the gate onto the unnamed trail and begin the ascent to Las Trampas Ridge. The trail climbs moderately through grassland and then turns right onto Las Trampas Ridge Trail, and continues for about 1½ miles with several curves, until the trail splits. Turn left, staying on Las Trampas Ridge Trail and begin the short loop that goes around Oak Circle. There are wide-open views of Mt. Diablo along the entire route.

Shortly, when the trail meets Sulphur Springs Trail, turn right and enjoy the shade as the trail dips down into a tiny valley with a cool stream and lots of greenery. It then climbs up and meets Del Amigo Trail. Turn right and finish the loop. Turn left on Las Trampas Ridge Trail and follow the trail down to the trailhead, bearing left onto the unnamed trail to Remington Loop. This is a gradual descent with beautiful views all the way down.

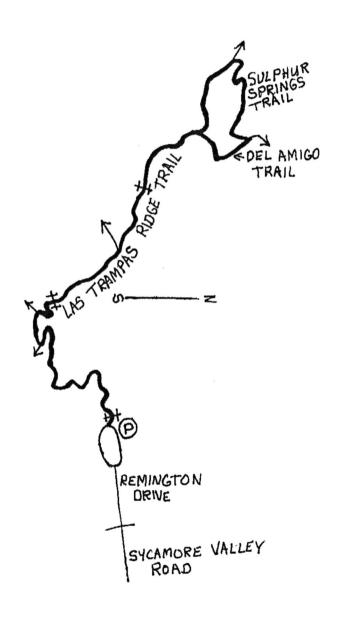

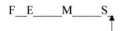

Las Trampas Regional Wilderness: Hike 10
Eagle Peak Trail

If you want a cardiovascular workout and great views, this is a wonderful hike! The trail climbs steadily until it reaches Eagle Peak. There are many old oak and Madrone trees that provide some welcome shade on a hot day. Be sure to bring a snack to munch on while relaxing on the bench at the top of Eagle Peak after a challenging climb.

Highlights:
- ❖ Great cardiovascular workout
- ❖ Stunning Diablo views
- ❖ Welcoming bench on peak
- ❖ 50% shade
- ❖ Option to convert to 1-way hike

Trail Details:
Distance: 6.2 miles
Time: 3 ½ hours
Altitude Gain: 1900'

Trail Map: East Bay Regional Park District – Las Trampas

Getting there: Follow directions to the South Avenue street parking.

The trail: The trail starts from South Avenue as a narrow steep footpath aptly named South Avenue Trail. Follow this trail under the shade of beautiful old oak and California bay trees for about 25 minutes until it intersects with Madrone Trail. Turn right and in a few minutes, the trail will continue both left and right. Turn left (this is still Madrone) and enjoy the views overlooking Mt. Diablo and the San Ramon Valley.

After a half mile, the trail meets Corduroy Hills Trail. Turn sharply right. The wide trail climbs up and gradually narrows into a footpath. This occurs at the bottom of the hill that leads to Eagle Peak. Bear to the right onto this trail (the trail also goes straight but loops back to the path) and continue climbing to the top. At the top, you will have climbed over 1700 feet, and your reward is a bench perched on the ridge, overlooking Mt Diablo.

Most of the return is downhill making it easier to enjoy the views. Retrace the hike back to South Avenue.

Option: To make this a 1-way hike, leave a car in the main Las Trampas parking lot. Follow the previous directions, but continue on Eagle Peak Trail to Las Trampas Ridge Trail. Turn left, then right on Chamise Trail to the bottom of the hill. Turn right on Bollinger Canyon Trail to the parking area. This reduces the hike by almost 2 miles.

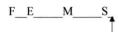

Las Trampas Regional Wilderness: Hike 11
Devil's Hole

This hike offers expansive views of San Francisco, the Sacramento River, Mt. Diablo, the Tri-Valley and the entire eastern ridge of Las Trampas Park. Climb a small path through typical California chaparral, ascend rock-topped ridges, and explore a beautiful canyon with large rock outcrops full of lichen. After a very steep climb, the trail traverses a ridge with wide-open views of Mount Diablo and the East Bay hills.

Highlights:
* Expansive views
* Good cardiovascular workout
* Creek bed with tree canopy
* Deep canyon
* Wind caves

Trail Details:
Distance: 6.5 miles
Time: 3 ½ hours
Altitude Gain: 1980'

Getting there: Park in the main Las Trampas parking lot.

The trail: Take Elderberry Trail at the south end of the parking lot. After a third mile, make a sharp right turn to stay on Elderberry Trail, and climb the fairly steep trail to the ridge. Turn right on Rocky Ridge View Trail and follow it for about a third mile to Devil's Hole Trail. Turn left and descend fairly steeply to Cull Creek. Just before reaching the creek, watch for a trail marker for Sycamore Trail. Turn right and walk a short distance to a shaded area with large branches to sit upon for a snack (watch carefully for poison oak). Proceed on Sycamore as it crosses the creek and leaves the shade.

The terrain now winds through typical arid California chaparral as the path climbs steeply to the first of three ridges. The trail drops into a beautiful canyon, climbs again to the second ridge, drops again and then makes a grand ascent – now through open grassland – to Rocky Ridge.

Turn left on Rocky Ridge View Trail, a narrow path paralleling a fenced-off road on the left. This is the high point of the park and has astounding views of the entire Bay Area. At the end of the ridge, it intersects with Rocky Ridge View Trail. Turn right and follow this to the paved road, also called Rocky Ridge View Trail. Stay on this or take the path to the left of the road that is slightly longer but more pleasant. Both return to the parking lot.

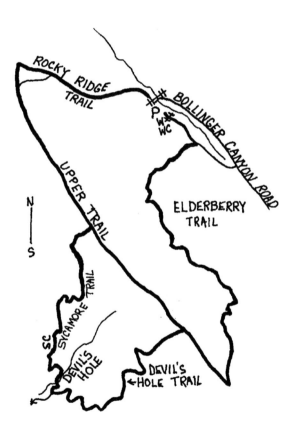

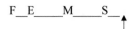
Las Trampas Regional Wilderness: Hike 12
East Side Loop

This is one of the most challenging of all the Tri-Valley hikes. It is also truly spectacular, as it crosses through several East Bay ecosystems showcasing a variety of plants, trees, flowers, grasses and views. You will travel in and out of canyons and across ridge tops that show off the best terrain of the park.

Highlights:	**Trail Details:**
❖ Large bay tree forest	Distance: 6.7 miles
❖ Deep shaded canyon	Time: 4 hours
❖ Ridge top hiking with views	Altitude Gain: 2500'

Trail Map: East Bay Regional Park District – Las Trampas

Getting there: Park in the main Las Trampas parking lot.

Trail description: Go over the bridge at the north end of the parking lot, cross the road, walk a short distance, then turn onto Bollinger Canyon Trail. Turn left on Chamise Trail. Watch for the Mahogany Trail marker and turn right. This leads deep into a shaded canyon. At the bottom, the trail crosses a wooden bridge and heads uphill. Shortly, take the right fork onto Trapline Trail, leading out of the canyon.

At the top of Las Trampas Ridge, Trapline intersects with the Las Trampas Ridge Trail. Turn right and enjoy the views as the trail flattens out and follows the ridge. Turn left on Del Amigo Trail after a half mile. This is a very steep downhill that can be treacherous in the summer as the trail turns to a powdery clay. Watch carefully for the Virgil Williams signpost on the left; it is off the trail and difficult to spot. Turn left on this pleasant trail which descends into a small shady canyon. Cross over Madrone Trail after the creek and continue right on Virgil Williams until it intersects with Madrone a second time. Turn right and after a few steps Madrone makes a sharp left turn and becomes quite steep.

84

When it levels out, it intersects with Corduroy Hills Trail. Bear left and continue upward. When the trail forks, take the footpath to the right and climb up to Eagle Peak on a small path for a well-deserved rest on the bench.

The remainder of the hike is much easier. Return to Corduroy Hills Trail, turn left, cross a saddle and go through the gate to Las Trampas Ridge Trail. Turn left and after half a mile go right on Chamise Trail. Shortly, go left on Mahogany that leads down into the northern section of the same canyon you started in. Mahogany leads out of the canyon; turn left on Chamise and walk to the bottom of the hill. Turn right on Bollinger Canyon Trail and follow it to the parking area across the road.

Los Vaqueros Watershed

Overview

Just beyond the northern boundaries of Livermore there is a new lake with over 50 miles of hiking trails. Years ago, several private ranches occupied this area. These disappeared when the Contra Costa Water District needed to improve the drinking water for their customers. A dam was built and the ranchland was flooded. This created a 1450-acre lake surrounded by 1850 acres of open space. There are two main entrances into the park, but it can also be accessed by hiking from Morgan Territory Regional Preserve or Round Valley Regional Park.

There is great variety in the trails, both in length and difficulty. From the Livermore entrance, there is one flat trail that runs along the lake for almost three miles, a couple of intermediate hikes and then some fairly strenuous hikes. One exceptional hike with unusual scenic vistas leaves from Morgan Territory; it is very steep but worth the effort. All of the hikes have a backdrop of cool blue lake water that contrasts with the warm golden hills.

The water district is exceptionally protective of the golden eagles in the park, sometimes closing the trails to hikers and always to dogs. These birds are very sensitive when incubating eggs and nurturing young chicks and adult birds may abandon them if disturbed. At first, it wasn't even clear that the trails would be open to the public, but naturalists solved this problem with random park closures.

Los Vaqueros may appear desolate and austere to newcomers. Although it is largely dry grassland with few trees at the lower levels, all of the trails have a unique view. The end of the flat lake trail, for example, is lushly green with a small creek emptying into the lake. Black Hills trail has a jaw-dropping moonscape-like vista. Experiment on some of the trails and spend a long day walking the entire length of the lake.

Los Vaqueros Watershed

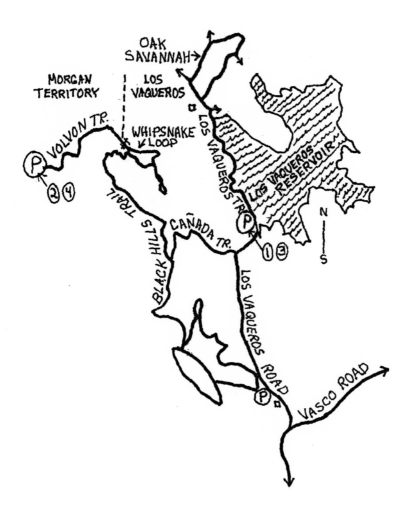

Directions to Los Vaqueros Watershed

Note that directions are from the intersection of Highways 580 and 680.

Take highway 580 east to the Vasco Road exit in Livermore. Turn north and drive for about three miles. Pass the Vasco Landfill on the right; then watch carefully for a small sign on the left for Los Vaqueros Watershed. Turn left (this is Los Vaqueros Road) and continue to the entrance booth. If this is closed, continue driving to the lake and pay for parking at the marina.

Note that at the time of this printing there is a $6 parking fee at the Vasco Road entrance. A $1 entrance fee is required if hiking from Morgan Territory. Exact change is required at both entrances.

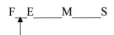

F E____M____S

Los Vaqueros Watershed: Hike 1
Los Vaqueros Trail

This almost flat trail offers a panoramic view of the new reservoir. It begins at the boat ramp then leads to the western tip of the lake where there is a beautiful creek passing old ranch buildings-a perfect spot for a picnic. The Badger Pass addition delves deeper into the park, using old ranch roads as the trail.

Highlights:
- Flat but scenic
- Lake side
- Old ranch buildings
- Winding creek
- Good children's hike

Trail Details:
Distance: 5.4 miles
Time: 2 hours
Altitude Gain: 100'

Trail Map: Los Vaqueros Watershed

Getting there: Go to the Los Vaqueros Watershed entrance. Pay the entrance fee, and continue on Los Vaqueros Road for three miles to the lake. Park in the parking lot at the marina.

The trail: Facing the marina building, walk to the left, heading toward the lake shore and get on Los Vaqueros Trail. It is often windy on this trail, and it can be muddy after a rainfall. Stroll along the lake for almost 3 miles and enjoy the many shorebirds such as white pelicans, grebes, mallards and coots. If you step carefully, you might spot a rare lily called Mission Bell; it is shaped like a rounded bell and is green with a yellow center underneath.

At the end of the lake, there is a beautiful feeder creek that cuts through grassland and winds around magnificent oaks. Enjoy this, as there are serious plans to deepen the lake and this area will be gone.

Return on the same trail.

90

Rainy day alternative: hike the trail that is slightly uphill and parallels Los Vaqueros Trail. It is a little hillier than the Los Vaqueros Trail. The footing is gravel for four miles, all the way to the boundary of Round Valley Regional Park. The trail comes to a barn at the end of the lake. Continue past the barn and turn right on Oak Savannah Trail. The gravel surface continues for almost another 2 miles.

Option: Instead of returning on the same trail, continue on Los Vaqueros around the ranch buildings and turn right at the first intersection onto Oak Savannah Trail. Turn right onto Badger Pass Trail and go through a gate. The trail makes a sharp turn to the right and then comes to another intersection. Stay right; there is a sign saying "to Los Vaqueros Trail". At the bottom of the hill, turn left onto the main trail and return to the parking area. This option adds about 2 miles and 250' altitude gain.

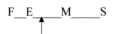
Los Vaqueros Watershed: Hike 2
Whipsnake Loop

This easy trail leads into the highest point and most spectacular area of the park, overlooking the entire reservoir. Beyond the reservoir, the expansive view opens up to the San Joaquin Valley and the Sierra Nevada Mountains. Since this trail begins high in Morgan Territory, rather than at the Los Vaqueros Watershed, the climb is done in the car, not by foot! Be sure to bring both the Morgan Territory and the Los Vaqueros maps.

Highlights:
- ❖ Expansive view
- ❖ Ponds
- ❖ Lush grassland

Trail Details:
Distance: 3.8
Time: 1½ hours
Altitude Gain: 450'

Trail Map: Los Vaqueros Watershed

Getting there: Park in the main Morgan Territory Regional Preserve parking lot to access Los Vaqueros from the west. (Do NOT go to the Los Vaqueros park entrance.)

The trail: Go through the gate, pass the trail on the left and go through the next gate; this is Volvon Trail. Climb a short hill, bear left, staying on Volvon. At the top of the hill it curves left and then right again as it descends slightly and passes a couple of ponds. The first intersection is Whipsnake Trail. Turn right. After about a quarter of a mile the trail comes to the entrance gate of Los Vaqueros. Pay the one-dollar fee and go through the gate.

Walk straight ahead and watch for the trail sign for Whipsnake Loop. Take the loop to the right and keep an eye out for deer running in and out among the trees. Continue circling to the left or take the short extension loop by bearing right at the next intersection. This loops back to the Whipsnake Loop trail. Continue walking, passing a beautiful pond on the left and finish the loop. Bear right on Whipsnake Trail, exit Los Vaqueros Watershed through the gate and retrace your steps back to the Volvon Trail intersection.

Turn right and after a few steps turn left which will keep you on Volvon. Watch carefully on the left for the next trail marker; this is Condor Trail. Turn left onto this narrow footpath and follow it through a clump of trees and then along a hillside. After almost a half mile, it dips and comes to a gate. Go through the gate (a pond is on the right) and continue on the trail back to the parking lot.

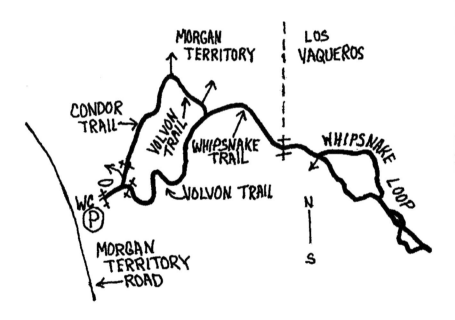

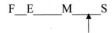
F__E____M____S

Los Vaqueros Watershed: Hike 3
Cañada Trail

This is a two-car caravan hike. The trail leads away from the lake to the interior grasslands of this old ranchland. The first two miles provide a good uphill workout that ends with spectacular views of the Sierra Nevada and the vast Central Valley. The lake is in view for most of the hike, providing a soothing contrast to the golden or green grasslands.

Highlights:
* ❖ Panoramic views
* ❖ Aerobic workout
* ❖ Lush green grasslands

Trail Details:
Distance: 5 miles
Time: 2 ¾ hours
Altitude Gain: 1400'

Trail Map: Los Vaqueros Watershed

Getting there: Leave one car in the parking lot to the left of the kiosk at the entrance to Los Vaqueros (P1 on the map). Take a second car another 3 miles and park in the marina parking lot by the lake (P2).

The trail: From the marina parking lot, walk back on the road a short distance. The beginning of Cañada Trail on the right is well marked. This trail climbs gradually uphill next to a wooded canyon for almost two miles before leveling out. There are usually nice breezes coming through the canyon although there is no tree cover for shade.

Bear left when the trail comes to Black Hills Trail. Shortly thereafter, climb to the top of the hill visible on the left (there is no trail). From there, the valley below stretches all the way to the Sierras—a spectacular view of the snowy peaks in winter.

Return to the trail. Black Hills Trail climbs a little again and then begins a long descent back to the first parking lot by the kiosk. There are a couple of intersecting trails so watch the trail signs. An endless stretch of green grassland is a highlight of this hike in the spring.

Los Vaqueros Watershed: Hike 4
Black Hills Trail

Black Hills Trail is easily accessed from Morgan Territory Regional Preserve. It is an unusual hike in that the first half is all downhill. Then the return, retracing the same trail, is totally uphill! There are incredible views of layered hills in the distance stretching to the Central Valley, as well as views of Los Vaqueros Reservoir and Brushy Peak. Be sure to have both Morgan Territory and Los Vaqueros maps for this hike.

Highlights:
❖ Panoramic view
❖ Long downhill
❖ Good workout
❖ Unique topography

Trail Details:
Distance: 6¼ miles
Time: 3½ hours
Altitude Gain: 1650'

Trail Map: Los Vaqueros Watershed

Getting there: Park in the main Morgan Territory parking lot to access Los Vaqueros from the west. (Do NOT go to the Los Vaqueros park entrance.)

The trail: Go through the gate, pass the trail on the left and go through the next gate onto Volvon Trail. Climb a short hill, bear left, staying on Volvon. The trail then descends and comes to an intersection with Whipsnake Trail. Stay right and after a few minutes, there is a gate with a sign in panel for Los Vaqueros Watershed (there is a one dollar fee). Go through the gate and bear right at the next turn. Watch carefully for the Black Hills Trail marker. The trail leads off to the right, passing through a gate. It curves back and forth a few times and comes to a crest.

The view is breathtaking for the next two miles as the trail descends straight down the ridge of a hill (try to forget that shortly you will have to climb back up this same hill)! There are no trees until the trail bottoms out at a beautiful creek. Sit under the canopy of oaks to rest up for the climb out.

Updates

Check out the Tri-Valley Trails website for updates at http://trivalleytrails.weebly.com.

Note that all parks in this book are dog friendly except Macedo Ranch (Mt. Diablo) and Los Vaqueros.

Page 22: should be 3 hours
Page 26: Switch starting points for #9 and 10
Page 74 – Should read: The trail bears right and becomes shaded with California bay trees. Pass a left turn trail sign for "to Las Trampas Peak" and Madrone Trail.
Page 101: as of April 2011, parking increased to $6
Page 102. Should read: Go through the gate by the restrooms and climb the small hill. At the first trail marker, turn right onto Wall Point Trail. It curves back and forth a few times, then comes to a gate. After the gate, there is another trail sign; Wall Point Trail turns to the right, but do not turn onto this trail. Instead go straight onto Dusty Road. The trail turns right, descends and comes to a sign for Stage Road. Turn left.
Page 105: The trail passes a shady picnic area, goes through a gate, and comes to the cattail-covered Pine Pond on the right before climbing out of the canyon. It then bends sharply right onto Dusty Road. Continue through the next gate onto Wall Point Trail. This eventually meets the main trail at the Briones Mt. Diablo/Summit Trail signpost. Turn left and descend the short distance to the parking area.
Page 110: Switch starting points for #5 and 10
Page 134: Switch starting points for #4 and 5
Page 144: should be 3½ hours
Page 152: Switch starting points for #5 and 6

You already know what to do - start climbing up Black Hills Trail! When you get to the top, retrace your steps back to Whipsnake Trail. When the trail intersects with Volvon Trail turn right rather than left. Watch for a hard-to-see trail marker for Condor Trail on the left. This narrow path leads along a hillside to a gate. Go through the gate and turn left. There will be a bucolic pond on the right. Continue and return to the parking area.

Macedo Ranch

Overview

Macedo Ranch is a staging area that provides access to the lower southwest hills of Mount Diablo State Park. It is mostly unknown to all but the locals in Danville. Trails with unique vegetation and geology are unlike others in this book. There are tree-shaded creeks, open views, interesting rock outcroppings and chaparral vegetation. Macedo Ranch also gives access to the higher flanks of Mt. Diablo and parks to the north such as Shell Ridge Open Space.

An old stagecoach road is the backbone of Macedo Ranch and its main trail. It crosses Pine Creek several times and is one of the shadiest trails in the region. Excellent examples of California creek side trees such as big leaf maple, sycamore and cottonwood are in abundance here. Children enjoy this park, as it is a perfect spot for wading and playing as the trail crosses the creek. A small picnic area is set aside under magnificent tall native trees with the creek close by for exploring.

For adults, Macedo Ranch is a good place for birding, as the trees and marsh plants supply the heavy foliage necessary for furtive flying friends. Don't forget to stop at Pine Pond on the way; it is home to a variety of waterfowl and tall marshy vegetation.

The hikes in this park can be shortened or lengthened by taking one of several trails connecting to Stage Trail or the higher trails in Mt. Diablo. Advanced hikers will find plenty of climbing on Summit Trail, which begins at Macedo Ranch and heads halfway up to the top of Mount Diablo.
The most unusual aspect of this trail is the large slabs of rock strewn about by geological activity. These frame perfect views of Morgan Territory and the lower Finley Road hills.

Macedo Ranch

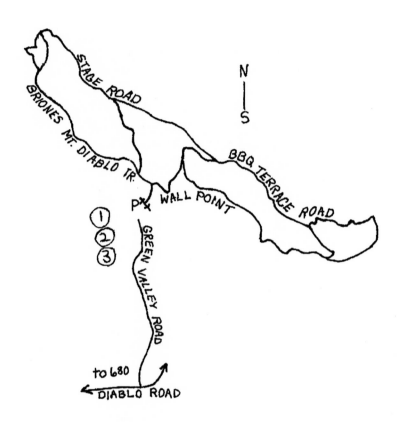

Directions to Macedo Ranch

Note that directions are from the intersection of Highways 580 and 680.

This is a staging area for Mount Diablo State Park. It is not part of East Bay Regional Park system. At the time of printing, there is a $3 parking fee.

Go north on 680 to Danville. Exit on Stone Valley Road. Pass the high school and turn left on Green Valley Road. Macedo Ranch is at the end of the road, about a mile from the turn.

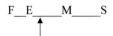

Macedo Ranch: Hike 1
Stage Road Trail

There is a special treat waiting at the bottom of the hill: Stage Road. Besides the history of being a real old stagecoach road, it has the feeling of another state; think Vermont, Michigan, Ohio. Huge trees cover the old road with shade, and some turn yellow in the fall. If this isn't enough, a creek runs along side the road and crosses it several times allowing for some creek fording.

Highlights:
- Heavy shade
- Wildflowers
- Creek

Trail Details:
Distance: 3 miles
Time: 1¼ hours
Altitude Gain: 450'

Trail Map: Mount Diablo State Park

Getting there: Park in the Macedo Ranch parking lot.

The trail: Go through the gate and climb the small hill. Turn right on Wall Point Trail. It dips, then curves right and comes to the intersection with Stage Road. Turn left and follow it downhill. The trail passes spring-fed Pine Pond with a wealth of vegetation. Take a few minutes to look for waterfowl and other birds. The trail levels off and begins to follow Pine Creek. Waterproof boots may help during the rainy season, as there are several creek crossings.

The trail leads into heavy shade under a canopy of bay, oak and water loving native trees. When Stage Road comes to a gate, go through it and to the left there is a well-shaded picnic table, a good place to stop for a snack. Continue your walk on Stage Road and turn left onto the narrow Yosemite Trail; it's only a short distance from the picnic table. The trail climbs up alongside a beautiful seasonal creek to open grassland and intersects with Briones Mt. Diablo Trail. Turn left and follow this back to the parking area.

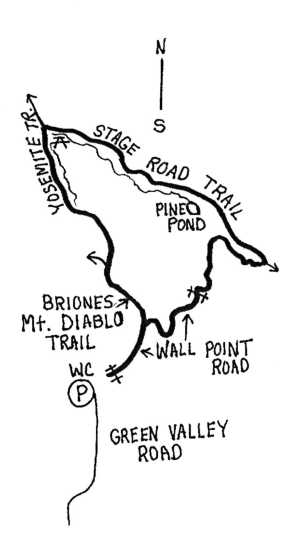

Macedo Ranch: Hike 2
Shell Loop Trail

The first part of this trail winds through lush green pastureland that magically transforms into golden hills in summer. The second half of the hike follows an old stagecoach road along the base of Mt. Diablo. A beautiful seasonal creek parallels the old road, crossing it many times. In the rainy season this can make the trail impassable because of all the creek crossings, and it can be quite muddy. If this is the case, turn around and retrace your steps to the Briones Mt. Diablo Trail and the parking area.

Highlights:
❖ Seasonal creek
❖ Shady picnic areas
❖ View of Castle Rock
❖ Fall color
❖ Many side trail options

Trail Details:
Distance: 6.5 miles
Time: 3 hours
Altitude Gain: 1000'

Trail Map: Mount Diablo State Park

Getting there: Park in the Macedo Ranch parking lot.

The trail: Go through the gate by the restrooms and begin a short climb to the Briones-Mt. Diablo/Summit Trail signpost. Stay straight, heading northwest, and climb up and down a variety of small hills in mostly open grassland. After a couple of miles, there is a gate and a trail sign straight ahead for Stonegate Trail to Walnut Creek Open Space. Turn right before reaching the gate. The trail becomes Shell Ridge Loop Trail.

When the trail meets Stage Road (also called Stage Trail), the return leg of this hike begins. Turn right and enjoy the most beautiful part of this hike. Look up to the left at the stunning rock formations of Castle Rock. Be awed by the towering bay, oak, and big leaf maple trees that cast dense shade over the old road. In the rainy season you may need to ford Pine Creek a few times as it breaches the road.

The trail passes a shady picnic area, goes through a gate, and comes to the cattail-covered Pine Pond on the right before climbing out of the canyon. It then bends sharply right, goes through another gate onto Wall Point Trail and eventually meets the main trail at the Briones Mt. Diablo/Summit Trail signpost. Turn left and descend the short distance to the parking area.

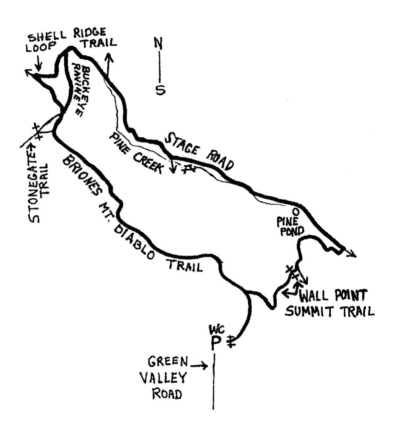

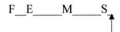

Macedo Ranch: Hike 3
Wall Point Trail

The base of Mt. Diablo is the setting for this hike. The first half climbs steadily through California chaparral with stunning rock formations. The climb to the summit is quite steep but ends with a panoramic view of the Mt. Diablo foothills, the valleys and beyond. The second half is downhill along a creek bed shaded with a variety of oak, buckeye and big leaf maple. Then a final push up out of the canyon leads back to the start.

Highlights:
❖ Aerobic workout
❖ Native chaparral landscape
❖ Panoramic views
❖ Seasonal creek
❖ Fall color

Trail Details:
Distance: 8 miles
Time: 3 ½ hours
Altitude Gain: 2150'

Trail Map: Mount Diablo State Park

Getting there: Park in the Macedo Ranch parking lot.

The trail: Go through the gate by the stone water trough, climb the hill and turn right when the trail splits. Go through the next gate and turn right again at the next fork; the trail sign will say "to Summit Trail". This is now Wall Point Road. Stay left at the next trail sign also marked "to Summit Trail".

After an hour, look left for the Ridge View Trail sign. This narrow trail leads straight up, about 300 feet, to the top of a grassy hill. Walk across the hill to the "Wall Point and to Summit" sign but go straight: don't turn right. The trail goes downhill to another sign for Summit Trail. Cross the road to the trail and turn left at the next sign "to BBQ Terrace". Cross the main road again onto a footpath. This path crosses two narrow paved roads, then through a wood gate onto a dirt road.

BBQ Terrace Road descends into a deep canyon and follows a creek bed bearing many native shade trees. After a mile, stay left at the trail sign "Stage Road to Diablo Foothills". Turn left again at the next sign "Dusty Road to Wall Point". Turn right at Wall Point Road, pass through the gate and when the road splits, stay left and continue back to the parking area.

Option: Turn left on Secret Trail to BBQ Terrace to reduce the hike by one hour and 850' elevation gain.

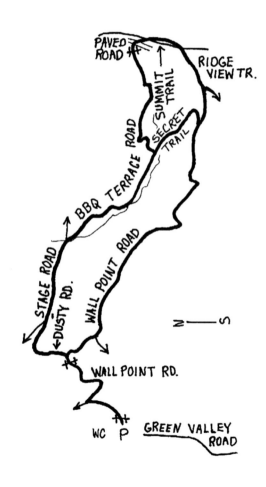

Morgan Territory Regional Preserve

Overview

Southeast of Mt. Diablo is the remote and quiet wilderness of Morgan territory. Most of the park is 2000 feet altitude or higher with spectacular views of the central valley and the snowy high Sierra. The name comes from a family of nineteenth century settlers who ranched in the area; descendants of that family still live close by. The access to the park is an adventure in itself, as the mostly one-lane road winds up from the valley floor. The park begins as the road reaches the summit and spreads out on both sides of Morgan Territory Road.

Morgan Territory covers a vast area that connects to Mt. Diablo State Park, Round Valley and Los Vaqueros. Hikers can wander for miles on old farm roads and trails that lead to beautiful creeks, steep ravines and high peaks. Many are sheltered by immense oak trees and pass seasonal creeks that tumble over moss-laden rocks used as mortars by the Native American Volvons long ago.

There are still many signs of early Volvon life in the park and the intrepid hiker only has to look for them. Several ancient grinding rocks can be found under acorn laden oaks that the Volvons would grind into flour and then mix with water from a nearby spring. A fifty foot rectangle of boulders found on a grassy knoll was a possible deer blind for capturing unsuspecting protein on hoof! Explore the vegetation in this park: toyon, coffeeberry, chamise, redberry, manzanita. Imagine how useful they might be to these early inhabitants.

History aside, this park has something for everyone, whether it is a short walk to a canyon overlook or a longer hike in search of the more than ninety varieties of wildflowers. It is a good all-season destination, too, as there are waterfalls and wildflowers in spring, shaded trails in summer, views of snow-covered peaks in winter, and a spectacular canopy of yellow leaves on the Mollok Trail in autumn.

.

Morgan Territory Regional Preserve

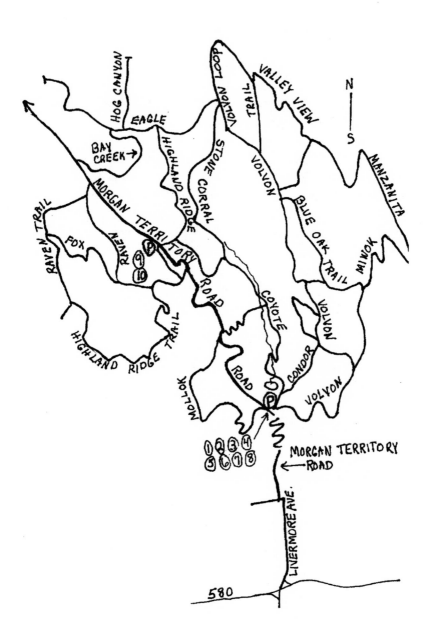

Directions to Morgan Territory Regional Preserve

Note that all directions are from the intersection of Highways 580 and 680.

Main Morgan Territory entrance: Take Highway 580 east. Exit at North Livermore Ave. Turn north. Follow North Livermore as it turns left and becomes Highland. Take the first right turn onto Morgan Territory Road. Drive 8.2 miles to the staging area on the right.

Highland Ridge Trailhead: Follow directions to main park entrance. Continue past the staging area about 2 ½ miles. Park on the side of the road near the gate at Highland Ridge Trail.

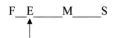

Morgan Territory Regional Preserve: Hike 1
Condor Trail

This short hike provides a good introduction into the beauty of this magnificent park. In late winter or early spring this is a great hike for a quick glimpse of some colorful spring wildflowers. It's a perfect hike for hesitant hikers such as novices and children.

Highlights:
- ❖ Mt. Diablo views
- ❖ Duck pond
- ❖ Short and scenic

Trail Details:
Distance: 1.3 miles
Time: ¾ hour
Altitude Gain: 100'

Trail Map: East Bay Regional Park District – Morgan Territory

Getting there: Park in the main Morgan Territory parking lot.

The trail: From the parking lot, go through the gate, pass the trail on the left and go through the next gate; this is Volvon Trail. Climb up a short hill and bear left, staying on Volvon. Turn left at the intersection with Whipsnake Trail, still staying on Volvon.

Shortly after that, when Blue Oak Trail splits to the right, go left on Volvon. After about ¼ mile (about 10 minutes), watch for a left turn onto Condor Trail. It is marked but easy to miss. This is a narrow footpath. Eventually Condor Trail leads down to a gate. Go through the gate and the trail borders a pond on the right shaded by a magnificent old oak tree. Follow the trail up the short hill and return to the parking area.

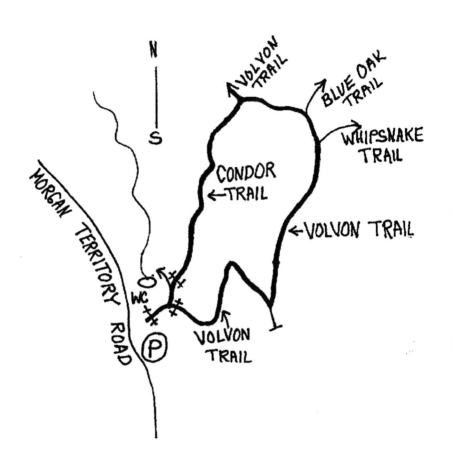

Morgan Territory Regional Preserve: Hike 2
Prairie Falcon

This is a short easy hike that shows off much of Morgan Territory's immense beauty. The trail meanders through a magnificent grove of native mature manzanita trees revealing their beautiful trunks. It continues through a dense thicket of low shrubs, typical of a California chaparral landscape. Enjoy the vast views from the overlook, and perhaps you will be lucky and spot a Peregrine Falcon or other raptor.

Highlights:
❖ Mt. Diablo views
❖ Manzanita grove
❖ Peregrine Falcons
❖ Canyon overlook
❖ Duck pond

Trail Details:
Distance: 2.6 miles
Time: 1½ hours
Altitude Gain: 150'

Trail Map: East Bay Regional Park District – Morgan Territory

Getting there: Park in the main Morgan Territory parking lot.

The trail: From the main parking lot., go through the gate, pass the trail on the left and go through the next gate; this is Volvon Trail. Climb up a short hill, bear left, staying on Volvon. Turn left at the intersection with Whipsnake Trail, still staying on Volvon. Shortly, turn right onto Blue Oak Trail. Notice that the shade cover increases with native blue oak trees, hence the name of the trail! Turn left on the very short Hummingbird Trail, and left again onto Volvon Trail.

Watch carefully now so you don't miss the small trail sign for Prairie Falcon Trail on the right. Turn onto Prairie Falcon, that takes you through a grove of colorful manzanita trees. Walk to the edge of the canyon overlook and enjoy the view while sitting on a rocky outcrop looking for raptors.

Continue on Prairie Falcon, turn right onto Volvon again and after a few steps, turn right on Condor Trail. This is also a narrow footpath with wildflower fields in the spring. Eventually the trail leads down to a gate. Go through the gate and the trail passes to the left of a pond where mallard ducks can often be seen in the springtime. Follow the trail up the short hill and return to the parking area.

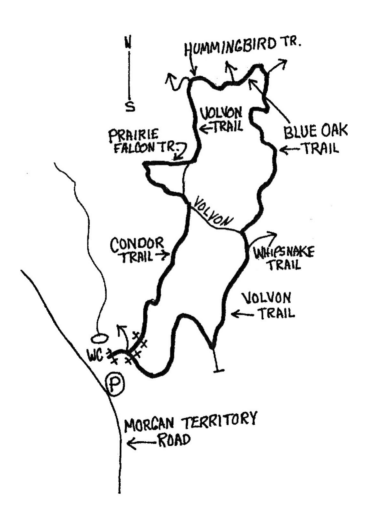

Morgan Territory Regional Preserve: Hike 3
Coyote Loop

Coyote Trail offers a rare sight in the Tri-Valley sun scorched hills; a heavily shaded trail that descends along a tumbling creek in winter and spring. There is spectacular wildflower viewing from late January to late May after a wet winter. Of note are large beds of Chinese Houses and Globe Lilies that carpet the hillside. An impressive boulder strewn creek drops more than five hundred feet to the valley floor.

Highlights:
- ❖ Wildflowers
- ❖ Part shade
- ❖ Tumbling creek

Trail Details:
Distance: 4.4 miles
Time: 2 hours
Altitude Gain: 700'

Trail Map: East Bay Regional Park District – Morgan Territory

Getting there: Park in the main Morgan Territory parking lot.

The trail: From the parking lot, go through the gate, walk a few feet and turn left on the next trail. This will lead to a pond. Follow the trail to the right of the pond and cross over the earthen dam. This is Coyote Trail. The trail turns right and descends along the west side of the creek. Later, it crosses the creek and follows the east side. The trail passes Mollok Trail on the left and then, as the trail levels off, watch for a gate. Go through it to Stone Corral Trail.

This is now open grassland. Stay on this trail until it intersects with Volvon Trail. Turn right and follow Volvon up the hill. The trail is now partially shaded by native oak trees. After a mile and a half, start looking for a trail marker for Condor Trail; turn right. This pleasant footpath follows the creek side trail that began this hike, but at a higher elevation.

After a small dip in the trail, there is a gate. Go through the gate and pass the pond on the right. Continue a short way on this trail to the parking area.

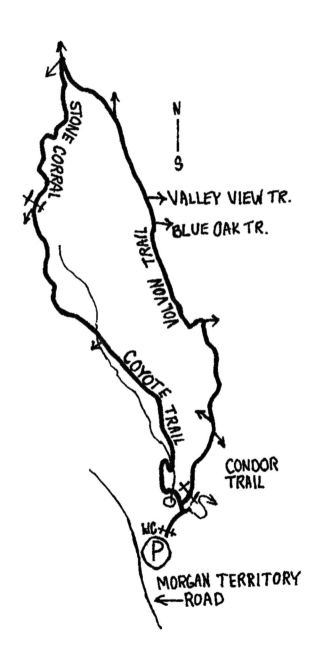

Morgan Territory Regional Preserve: Hike 4
Clyma Trail

Beat the summer heat with this mostly shady trail that descends almost entirely for the first 2 miles into a deep canyon. The last mile is straight uphill for about 800 feet but also very shady. In winter, spring and into early summer an unbelievably beautiful creek tumbles over large mossy boulders just below the narrow trail. Since this trail is on a western slope, peepholes of sun poke through the leaves encouraging a great variety of wildflowers quite late into the summer.

Highlights:
❖ Lots of shade
❖ Spring wildflowers
❖ Tumbling creek

Trail Details:
Distance: 2.7 miles
Time: 1 ¾ hours
Altitude Gain: 800'

Trail Map: East Bay Regional Park District – Morgan Territory

Getting there: Park in the main Morgan Territory parking lot.

The trail: From the parking lot, go through the small gate at the northwest end and cross over Morgan Territory Road. Clyma Trail begins here. Stay on this trail, passing the right turn to Mollok Trail.

Eventually the trail makes a sharp turn to the right and ascends slightly to open grassland. Clyma now turns right, and descends to Mollok Trail. Turn left and continue to descend into the canyon, crossing the road and winding through the oak shaded woods. At the bottom, turn right onto Coyote Trail, following the creek, climbing steeply back to the parking lot.

Option: Reverse this hike to avoid the steep uphill at the end. The total altitude gain remains the same.

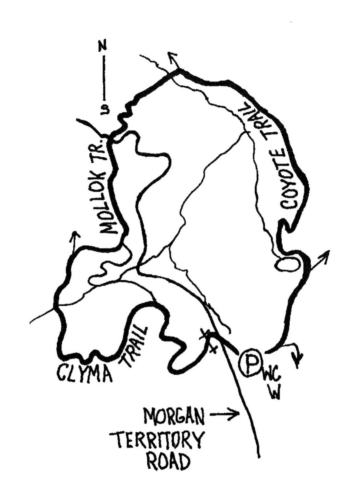

N

S

MOLLOK TR.

COYOTE TRAIL

CLYMA TRAIL

P WC
W

MORGAN →
TERRITORY
ROAD

Morgan Territory Regional Preserve: Hike 5
Raven Trail

This is an up and down trail with a lot of variety in the terrain. Although most of the trail is in the open, there are many shady creek side places to cool down. This trail wanders on both sides of Morgan Territory Road into less traveled areas of the park. Don't miss the stands of big leaf maple trees that turn brilliant yellow in mid October.

Highlights:
* Fall color
* Seasonal creeks
* Varied terrain

Trail Details:
Distance: 3.5 miles
Time: 1¾ hours
Altitude Gain: 1000'

Trail Map: East Bay Regional Park District – Morgan Territory

Getting there: Park at the Highland Ridge Trailhead.

The trail: Enter the gate on the east side of the road onto Highland Ridge Trail. Shortly the trail climbs out into open grassland and continues climbing up 400 feet to the intersection with Eagle Trail. Turn left and after about 1/3 mile turn left again onto Bay Creek Trail.

This trail makes a long descent along a seasonal creek. Notice the pungent smell of native bay trees that shade this part of the trail early in the day. The creek also provides moisture to satisfy the demands of the Big Leaf Maples that are most apparent in the fall.

The trail ends at Morgan Territory Road. Climb over the fence, if locked, turn left and walk up the road for about three minutes and watch for the vehicle gate on the right. Climb over this gate, also, if locked, and you will be on Raven Trail. Stay left at the fork, following Raven for about ½ mile and a 500' climb to the highest point in this hike. Turn left onto Fox Trail. After about

1/10 mile, there is a Highland Ridge Trail sign up to the left, off of the trail. Turn left at this intersection. The trail goes downhill and then splits. A sign post says, "Diablo Regional Trail and Highland Ridge Trail." Take the left turn and follow this a quarter mile down to your car.

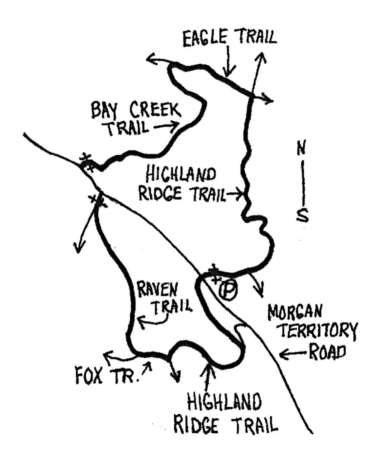

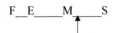
Morgan Territory Regional Preserve: Hike 6
Manzanita Trail

The eastern side of Morgan Territory is reached by this deep canyon trail. It starts with a steady descent to a seasonal creek, lined with mature big leaf maple and bay trees. The trail leads out of the canyon, climbing steadily. At the top, it reveals panoramic views of Los Vaqueros Reservoir and the snow-capped Sierra Nevada beyond. This hike is a good choice for summer, as half of its length is shaded with a variety of native trees.

Highlights:
- ❖ Panoramic views
- ❖ Pretty ponds
- ❖ Aerobic but not steep
- ❖ Seasonal creek
- ❖ Shade

Trail Details:
Distance: 5 ½ miles
Time: 2 ¼ hours
Altitude Gain: 850'

Trail Map: East Bay Regional Park District – Morgan Territory

Getting there: Park in the main Morgan Territory parking lot, go through the gate, pass the trail on the left and go through the next gate; this is Volvon Trail. Climb up a short hill, bear left, staying on Volvon. Turn left at the intersection with Whipsnake Trail, still staying on Volvon.

Shortly after that, turn right onto Blue Oak Trail. Be sure to take in the gorgeous views of Mt. Diablo! At the next intersection bear right onto Miwok Trail (Blue Oak Trail goes off to the left) and descend for a few minutes. Make a hairpin left onto Manzanita, still descending steadily to the creek. The trail then ascends for about 20 minutes, until you reach an intersection with Valley View Trail, where you turn left. After about 10 minutes, there is a T intersection; turn left and go through the gate (there is an outhouse there). After one minute turn left onto

Blue Oak. Don't miss the beautiful vistas to the left, overlooking Los Vaqueros Reservoir.

A few minutes later pass a seasonal pond on the left (a great spot to cool down for dogs!). Stay on Blue Oak passing the turnoff for Hummingbird Trail. When you reach a fork in the road, go left onto Volvon and continue to the parking lot.

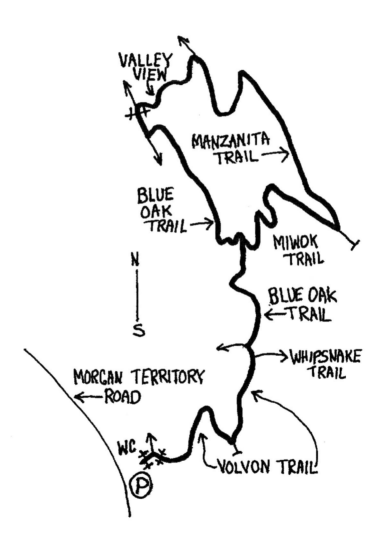

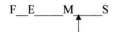

Morgan Territory Regional Preserve: Hike 7
Volvon Loop Trail

Expansive views of Mt. Diablo dominate this entire hike. The trail is fairly level for the first two hours, followed by a moderate climb. Volvon Trail stretches along the length of the park, north/south, and stays pretty much to the top of the ridge. This is exquisite savanna land; open grassland dotted with native oak, manzanita and buckeye trees.

Highlights:
- ❖ Mt. Diablo views
- ❖ Sierra Nevada views
- ❖ Ridge top hiking

Trail Details:
Distance: 5.7 miles
Time: 3 hours
Altitude Gain: 1100'

Trail Map: East Bay Regional Park District – Morgan Territory

Getting there: Park in the main Morgan Territory parking lot.

The trail: From the main parking lot, go through the gate, pass the trail on the left and go through the next gate; this is Volvon Trail. Climb up a short hill. Bear left, staying on Volvon. Turn left at the intersection with Whipsnake Trail, still staying on Volvon.

After a few feet, turn right onto Blue Oak Trail. The scenery begins to open up to reveal the vast expanses of northern California ranching country. This typical tree-studded savanna with gentle slopes is good for grazing and hiking!

Turn right when Blue Oak ends at Volvon. Be sure to notice the perfect examples of native blue oak and buckeye trees that provide occasional shade. After ¼ mile turn right on Volvon Loop Trail that circles Bob Walker Ridge and continue to the northern end of the park. Look to the right for a spectacular view of the Central Valley and Sierra Nevada.

Continue on the Volvon Loop Trail, staying left on Volvon when the trail splits. The trail now climbs back to the ridge. Follow Volvon for about 1½ miles and then begin watching on the right for the Condor Trail marker (if you miss it, just continue on Volvon to the parking lot) and turn right. Follow this scenic narrow path until it comes to a gate. Go through the gate, bear left, go around the pond and return to the parking lot.

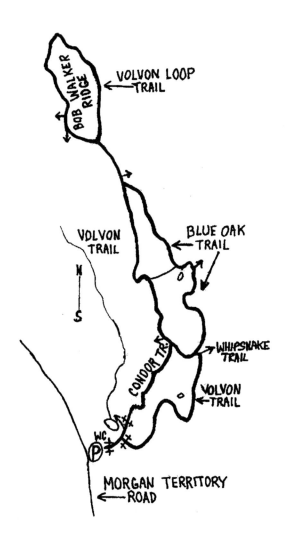

Morgan Territory Regional Preserve: Hike 8
Valley View Trail

This is a "top of the world" hike as it stays mostly atop the higher elevations of the east side of Morgan Territory Park. The trail affords spectacular vistas of the central valley and the Sierra Nevada mountain range. Winter is the best time for this hike, as the air is clear and the snow capped peaks come into view.

Highlights:
* Sierra Nevada view
* Los Vaqueros lake view
* Wildflowers

Trail Details:
Distance: 6.1 miles
Time: 2 ¾ hours
Altitude Gain: 1300'

Trail Map: East Bay Regional Park District – Morgan Territory

Getting there: Park in the main Morgan Territory parking lot.

The trail: Begin on the east side of the main parking lot. Go through the gate, pass the trail on the left and go through the next gate; this is Volvon Trail. Climb up a short hill, bear left, staying on Volvon. Turn left at the intersection with Whipsnake Trail, still staying on Volvon.

Shortly after that, turn right onto Blue Oak Trail, staying on this until it once again meets Volvon. Be careful not to turn onto any other intersecting trails. Turn right on Volvon and after a few steps, turn right on Valley View Trail. Fairly quickly, this trail will descend into a canyon, cross a seasonal creek and then climb back to the ridge. Turn right on Volvon Loop Trail (also called Bob Walker Ridge Trail).

At the very tip of this trail, you will be at the northernmost part of the east side of this park. Walk on the narrow path to the clump of trees for a snack or continue out to the tip of the ridge for a look into the canyon below. Then return to the main trail and continue to the west side of Volvon Loop trail as it goes

126

around Bob Walker Ridge. Bear left onto Volvon Trail and continue for a little over a mile and a half to Condor Trail. There is a trail marker where this meets Volvon, but it is easy to miss. Turn right and enjoy this scenic footpath as it leads to a gate. Go through the gate, bear left and return to the parking lot.

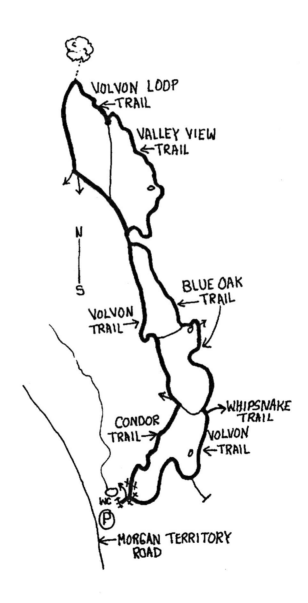

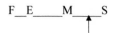
Morgan Territory Regional Preserve: Hike 9
Highland Ridge Trail

This trail has unbelievable views and provides a great workout! After a mile and a half of steady climbing, this trail levels off on top of a ridge that offers spectacular panoramic views of the San Ramon Valley to the left and the eastern ridge of the park to the right. In the distance, the views stretch further to the Carquinez Strait and the Sierras. The trail then traverses into interior hills that are fairly untrammeled, making a great getaway for the fit hiker! This sunny hike is best when it isn't too hot.

Highlights:
* Great aerobic workout
* Panoramic views
* Ridge top hiking
* Open savanna

Trail Details:
Distance: 4.2 miles
Time: 2 hours
Altitude Gain: 1250'

Trail Map: East Bay Regional Park District – Morgan Territory

Getting there: Park at the Highland Ridge Trail trailhead.

The trail: Cross to the west side of the road and go through the gate. You are now on Highland Ridge Trail. The trail immediately begins climbing through a grove of oak trees. Shortly, it leaves the shade for open savanna. Continue climbing for approximately ten more minutes when the trail dips slightly and intersects with Raven Trail. Turn left, continuing on Highland Ridge Trail until you reach the top of the ridge. The view opens up at the same time as the trail levels off, so that you can enjoy the sights while easing your pace.

After this short trek along the ridge, the trail begins to descend and meets Raven Trail. Turn right and continue downward until it intersects with Fox Trail. Make a sharp hairpin right turn and follow Fox Trail back to the intersection with Raven Trail. Be sure to go right on Raven and not left. Turn left onto Highland

Ridge Trail and after about five minutes bear left to stay on Highland Ridge, and follow it back to the parking area.

This trail is well marked with sign posts which are helpful, as it is easy to make a wrong turn on several of the intersections.

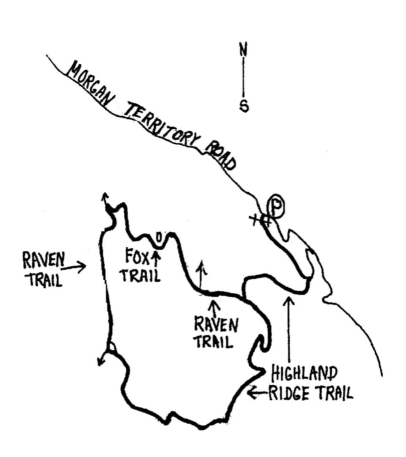

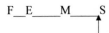
Morgan Territory Regional Preserve: Hike 10
Eagle Trail

This hike covers a good portion of the park. The trail begins almost level then drops down to the main canyon, sliced by a beautiful creek and tumbling boulders. At the northern end of the trail, the grade changes to a steep climb out of the cool shade and then quickly descends to the creek level again, ending with another climb out of the same shady canyon up to your car.

Highlights:
* Shade
* Creeks
* Indian grinding rocks
* Aerobic workout

Trail Details:
Distance: 7.9 miles
Time: 3 hours
Altitude Gain: 1400'

Trail Map: East Bay Regional Park District – Morgan Territory

Getting there: Park in the main Morgan Territory parking lot.

The trail: Go through the small gate at the northwest end of the parking lot and cross over Morgan Territory Road to Clyma Trail. Stay on Clyma, passing the right turn to Mollok Trail. Eventually Clyma Trail makes a sharp turn to the right and ascends slightly to open grassland. The trail then turns right, and descends to Mollok Trail. Turn left and follow the trail to the road; cross the road, descending under oak shaded woods.

At the bottom, cross the creek and turn left onto Coyote Trail. It traverses open grassland and has remnants of ancient Indian grinding rocks along the way. Turn left onto shady Stone Corral Trail and turn right when it intersects with Highland Ridge Trail. Go right again at the intersection with Eagle Trail, and now the steep climb begins. Stop for a breath at the top and then decide whether to take the easy way back or face another grueling, but rewarding, climb back to your car.

The more challenging, and more scenic way, is to turn right on Volvon, then almost immediately bear right onto Stone Corral. After .6 mile, turn left on Coyote Trail. This is easy in the beginning but ends with a 400' climb. Luckily, it is all under cover of oak trees and follows a cascading creek in winter.

The easier way is to stay on Volvon Trail after leaving Eagle Trail and follow it to the parking lot. This reduces the total climb by 400'.

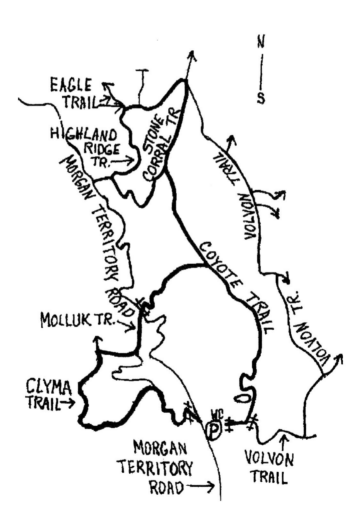

Pleasanton Ridge Regional Park/
Augustin Bernal Park

Overview

Pleasanton Ridge Regional Park and the much smaller Augustin Bernal Park have the perfect formula for ridge-top hiking. Although the staging areas begin close to the valley floor, most of the trails are up along the ridge. The two adjacent parks cover most of the Pleasanton ridge, located west of Highway 680. Four main trails, Ridgeline, North Ridge, Thermalito and Sinbad Creek, run almost the full north-south length of the parks and can all be accessed from both parks. Dramatic vistas of the Diablo and Hamilton mountain ranges and Mission Peak are the backdrop for the entire Tri-Valley below.

The trails on the east side are the ones with grand vistas but they can be somewhat noisy from the freeway 1000 feet below. The western ridge on the other hand, overlooks Kilkare Canyon and Sunol Ridge and is quiet and pastoral. An alternative to these ridgeline trails is Sinbad Creek Trail that follows a heavily wooded riparian canyon with a stunning creek, and then leads north into a newer acquisition of the park.

Grassland dominates the vegetation in Pleasanton Ridge (an East Bay Regional park) and this supports an abundant variety of wildflowers from late winter through spring. Beautiful displays of tarweed can be seen surrounding some of the park's many cow ponds even in late summer. Native trees tend to clump together on the west side of Pleasanton Ridge. In the south end of the park, up on the ridge, trails pass through old olive groves. These were planted a hundred years ago and rangers are working to restore them. Most of Augustin Bernal Park (owned by the city of Pleasanton) is richly covered in oak woodland savannahs and dense forests.

Pleasanton Ridge's over 4000 acres are growing with new land purchases from local ranchers. Although it takes a while for trails to materialize on these new land acquisitions, it will be worth the wait. Someday there may be trails all the way from Pleasanton Ridge to Las Trampas!

Pleasanton Ridge Regional Park/Augustin Bernal Parks

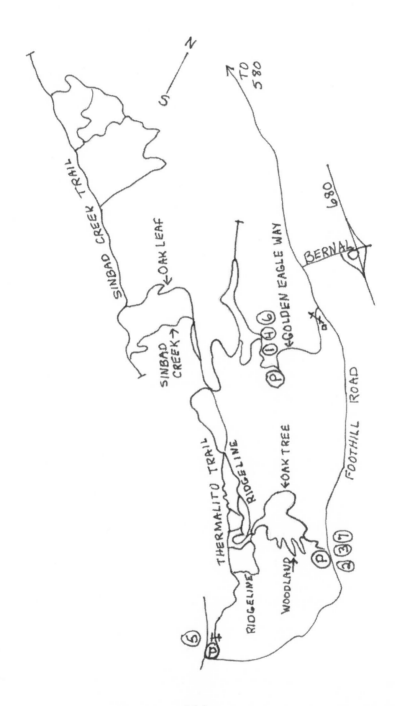

Directions to Pleasanton Ridge Regional Park/Augustin Bernal Parks

Note that all directions are from the intersection of Highways 580 and 680.

Oak Tree Staging Area:
Take highway 680 south. Exit at Castlewood Drive/Sunol Blvd and turn right (west). Turn left on Foothill Road. Continue to the staging area on the right.

Sunol entrance:
Take highway 680 south. Exit at highway 84 and turn right on Paloma Road. Turn right on Main Street, just after the first intersection. Turn right on Kilkare Road and immediately turn right into the public parking lot across from the train station. Walk over the tracks and turn right on the road adjacent to the tracks. Turn left on the first street. This narrow road leads into Pleasanton Ridge Regional Park.

Golden Eagle parking lot (Augustin Bernal Park):
Note that Pleasanton residents must show proof of residency before entering this area. Non-residents are required to have a permit, which can be obtained from the Pleasanton parks and Community Services Offices behind the Pleasanton Library.

Take highway 680 south. Exit on Bernal Avenue and turn right (west). Turn left on Foothill Road and right on Golden Eagle Way. Show your permit at the guard gate and continue to the parking area.

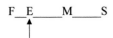

Augustin Bernal Park: Hike 1
Valley View Trail

This circular trail is a good hike for beginners or for those who just want a short trek in the wilderness. There are a variety of native California trees along the way plus some good birding opportunities along Chaparral Trail. This hike begins with a short ascent of 350 feet, or it can be done in reverse for a more gradual, but longer climb.

Highlights:
❖ Several varieties of native oak
❖ Mostly shady

Trail Details:
Distance: 2 ¼ miles
Time: 1 hour
Altitude Gain: 350'

Trail Map: City of Pleasanton – Augustin Bernal Park

Getting there: Park in the Golden Eagle parking lot. Note that a permit is required for non-Pleasanton residents.

The trail: Leave the sycamore-shaded parking area and go through the gate. This puts you on Golden Eagle Trail. Turn left after a half-mile onto Chaparral Trail. You will see plenty of its namesake along the way plus the not-so-friendly poison oak.

When the trail intersects with Valley View Trail, turn right. Now relax as the trail slowly descends. After a mile, Valley View makes a hairpin turn to the right. Try to identify the variety of native oaks visible along this trail: coast live oak, blue oak, and black oak. Stay on Golden Eagle Trail to the parking area where there are picnic tables waiting for you!

Option: When Valley View Trail makes a right hairpin turn, bear left onto Toyon Trail, then right on Longview Trail. This merges with Golden Eagle Trail and returns to the parking area. This option adds about .4 mile, ½ hour and 50 feet altitude gain.

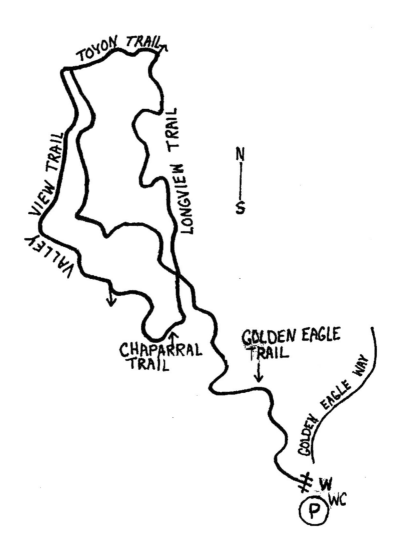

TOYON TRAIL

LONGVIEW TRAIL

VIEW TRAIL

VALLEY

N
S

GOLDEN EAGLE
TRAIL

CHAPARRAL
TRAIL

GOLDEN EAGLE WAY

W
WC
P

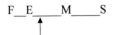

Pleasanton Ridge Regional Park: Hike 2
Woodland Trail

This short hike provides access to the ridge, the main part of the park. It gives a glimpse of native vegetation and provides a quick workout. The first part of the hike on Oak Tree Trail climbs steadily to the ridge. Woodland Trail is a rugged footpath with lots of foliage and trees. These native oaks provide sun shelter on a hot summer day.

Highlights:
- ❖ Short cardiovascular hike
- ❖ Native woodland
- ❖ Shade

Trail Details:
Distance: 2.3 miles
Time: 1 ¼ hours
Altitude Gain: 600'

Trail Map: East Bay Regional Park District – Pleasanton Ridge

Getting there: Park in the Oak Tree Staging Area.

The trail: From the parking lot, go through the gate beyond the outhouses and begin walking up Oak Tree Trail. It veers to the right and then almost turns back on itself as it climbs up to the ridge. When the trail levels out at the top of the ridge, look carefully left for the Woodland Trail sign. Turn left onto this narrow trail and follow it down through oak woodland with typical native undergrowth of wildflowers and shrubs. Eventually the trail intersects with Oak Tree Trail. Turn right and head back to the parking area.

138

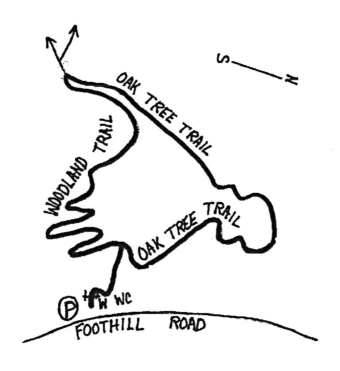

Pleasanton Ridge Regional Park: Hike 3
Olive Grove Trail

This loop hike provides an overview of what this park has to offer. The views are spectacular even with the freeway trailing along the valley below. The canyon side of the trail leads into the remote area of the park with open grassland, ponds and wildflowers. A little history of early settlers comes to mind while walking among the perfectly preserved hundred-year-old olive groves.

Highlights:
❖ Valley and canyon views
❖ Ridgeline hiking
❖ Old olive grove

Trail Details:
Distance: 4.8 miles
Time: 1 ¾ hours
Altitude Gain: 1050'

Trail Map: East Bay Regional Park District – Pleasanton Ridge

Getting there: Park in the Oak Tree Staging Area.

The trail: Go through the gate beyond the outhouses and begin hiking on Oak Tree Trail. This is a steady climb up a somewhat open road. At the summit there is a fork. Take the right arm of the fork uphill; this is Ridgeline Trail. This trail circles the knoll, then begins following the ridge with a vista overlooking Pleasanton to the east. Shortly, turn left at the trail marker that says "to Olive Grove Trail", then bear right onto Olive Grove Trail. It will be obvious how the trail got its name.

Stay on this trail until it intersects with Ridgeline Trail once again. Turn left and continue about a half-mile, then make a sharp left hairpin turn onto Thermalito Trail. A deep canyon now comes into view on the right with Sunol Ridge forming the western side of the park. This is the quiet side of the park with rolling hills, seasonal ponds and open grassland.

Watch for the "to Olive Grove Trail" sign on the left and take this trail back to Olive Grove Trail and turn right. Turn right on Ridgeline Trail and follow it around the knoll. Straight ahead, the trail splits with Oak Tree Trail to the left and Woodland Trail to the right. Turn right onto this narrow shady footpath, then right when Woodland Trail ends at Oak Tree Trail.

Option: Continue on Ridgeline as far as you like beyond Thermalito Trail, then retrace your steps, turn right on Thermalito and follow the directions above.

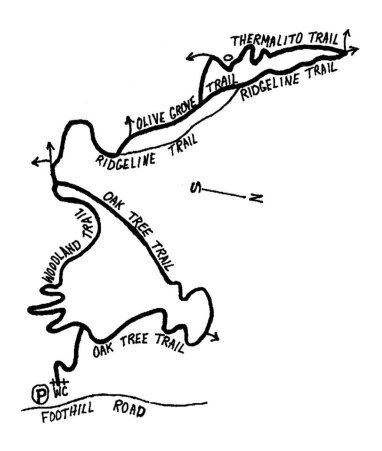

Pleasanton Ridge Regional Park: Hike 4
Sunol Thermalito Trail

The relatively unknown access to Pleasanton Ridge Park, leaves from the picturesque town of Sunol. The first half of the hike climbs the eastern flank of Kilkare Canyon. This is a beautiful and quiet canyon with open hills, native oaks and vintage olive groves. The second half of the hike is mostly downhill and also traverses the ridge top, offering distant views of the hills of Sunol, Apperson Ridge and the Ohlone wilderness.

Highlights:
* Expansive view
* Gradual climb
* Several ponds
* Lunch in Sunol

Trail Details:
Distance: 5 miles
Time: 2 ½ hours
Altitude Gain: 1250'

Trail Map: East Bay Regional Park District – Pleasanton Ridge

Getting there: Park in the Sunol Entrance.

The trail: Cross over the train tracks and turn right on the road that parallels the tracks. Turn left on the first street and climb up to the entrance gate. This is Thermalito Trail. It climbs gradually through mostly open grazing land with very little shade.

Take the first right turn at the signpost for Ridgeline Trail. Stay on Ridgeline for a half-mile of steep climbing. When the trail levels off, turn left on Oak Tree Trail. Then turn right on Thermalito, a trail that rolls up and down, in and out of shade and follows beautiful Kilkare Canyon.

Turn right on Olive Grove Trail, then left on Ridgeline Trail. This trail skirts the east side of the ridge, opening up spectacular views of the Tri-Valley. It comes to an intersection with Thermalito again. Make the sharp hairpin turn left and follow this trail back about a mile and a half to the gate at the beginning of this hike. Go through the gate, down the road and return to the parking area.

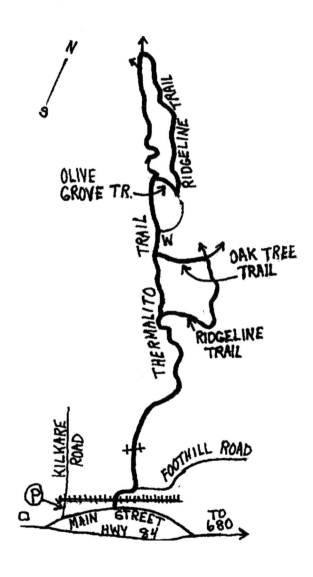

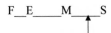

Pleasanton Ridge Regional Park/Augustin Bernal:
Hike 5-Bay Leaf Trail

This hike descends into the interior canyon of the park and gives a snapshot of Sinbad Creek. There are beautiful specimens of ancient native oaks, bay, big leaf maple, sycamore and the smaller toyon and elderberry trees. From late winter through spring much of this trail is dazzled with wildflowers and reeded ponds. Two climbs, one in and one out, provide plenty of exercise along with this beauty.

Highlights:
❖ Riparian creek
❖ Panoramic views
❖ Large ponds
❖ Aerobic workout

Trail Details:
Distance: 7.3 miles
Time: 2 ½ hours
Altitude Gain: 1300'

Trail Map: East Bay Regional Park District – Pleasanton Ridge and City of Pleasanton – Augustin Bernal Park

Getting there: Park in the Golden Eagle parking lot. Note that a permit is required for non-Pleasanton residents.

The trail: Take Golden Eagle Trail from the parking area and turn left onto Chaparral Trail. Turn left again when it intersects with Valley View Trail. This leads to the top of Pleasanton Ridge. Turn right on Ridgeline Trail, go through a gate and bear right. Turn left on Sinbad Creek Trail; a pleasant descent to Kilkare Canyon and Sinbad Creek. Turn right, staying on Sinbad Creek Trail, and meander along the creek and enjoy the shade and riparian vegetation, so rare in the Tri-Valley anymore. Look for the mottle-barked sycamores along the creek.

Continue along the creek until reaching a trail marker for Bay Leaf Trail. Turn right on this trail and climb out of the canyon to the open grassland on the ridge. This becomes

144

Ridgeline Trail. Stay right after reaching the top and pass along a pond on the right. Bear left when the trail splits just after the Sinbad Creek Trail intersection staying on Ridgeline, and after a half mile, go through the gate. This is still Ridgeline Trail so continue another third of a mile and turn left on Valley View Trail. Watch for the Chaparral Trail shortcut on the right and follow this path until it intersects with Golden Eagle Trail. Turn right and continue descending to the parking area.

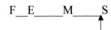

Pleasanton Ridge Regional Park/Augustin Bernal Park:
Hike 6 - Sinbad Creek Trail

This trail rests in the lower part of the parks in Kilkare Canyon, between Pleasanton Ridge and Sunol Ridge. The creek meanders for several miles along the canyon floor, and the trail follows it until it meets Kilkare Road. To get to the canyon floor, you must first climb to the Ridge then walk down into the heavily wooded riparian creek. Since this area escaped extensive grazing so typical of the Tri-Valley hills, there is a spectacular sense of descending back in time.

Highlights:
- Native creek vegetation
- Heavy shade
- Large ponds
- Aerobic workout

Trail Details:
Distance: 11 miles
Time: 4 ¾ hours
Altitude Gain: 1400'

Trail Map: East Bay Regional Park District – Pleasanton Ridge and City of Pleasanton – Augustin Bernal Park

Getting there: Park in the Golden Eagle parking lot. Note that a permit is required for non-Pleasanton residents.

The trail: Go through the gate and begin walking on Golden Eagle Trail. After a half-mile, turn left onto Chaparral Trail, a shady shortcut to Valley View Trail. Turn left onto Valley View and climb to the ridge. Turn right on Ridgeline Trail. It follows the ridge and leads to two trails that drop into Kilkare Canyon passing some beautiful ponds in the spring. Bear either right or left when the trail splits, as they parallel each other. Pass the sign to Sinbad Creek Trail, continue a third mile and turn left on Bay Leaf Trail. Immediately begin descending into the canyon, leaving the open woodland behind.

About half way down, Bay Leaf Trail becomes densely shaded; an indication of the trail to come. At the bottom of the canyon, cross the creek and turn right on Sinbad Creek Trail. Look carefully at the moss covered trees and the dense undergrowth. The creek eventually narrows and the trail ascends out of this riparian area into open grassland. Notice the two ridges on either side of the trail that drain down the slopes and fill the creek.

The trail ends at a gate to private land. Return the same way you came, taking in a reverse view of the grand scenery and cooling those now aching feet in the creek.

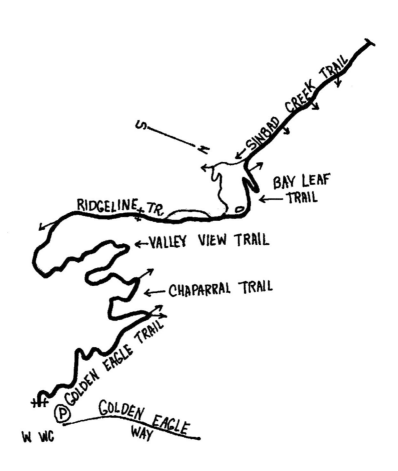

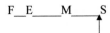
Pleasanton Ridge Regional Park: Hike 7
Ridgeline Trail

There are two parallel trails that go along the top of Pleasanton Ridge. Both have knockout views of the whole Tri-Valley and the surrounding mountains. The trail roller coasters up and down almost the whole distance of this hike, providing a good workout to compliment the views. The return trail passes under an umbrella of native oak trees and passes several year round ponds.

Highlights:
- ❖ Panoramic views
- ❖ Anaerobic workout
- ❖ Ponds
- ❖ Old olive groves

Trail Details:
Distance: 7.9 miles
Time: 4 hours
Altitude Gain: 1700'

Trail Map: East Bay Regional Park District – Pleasanton Ridge

Getting there: Park in the Oak Tree Staging Area.

The trail: Go through the gate and follow Oak Tree Trail up the hill. Straight ahead there is a fork. Take the right arm of the fork uphill; this is Ridgeline Trail. It turns back to the right and then pretty much follows the ridge in a northwest direction, going up and down quite a few hills. Always check the trail signs at the intersections, so that you don't inadvertently stray off Ridgeline. A strategically placed picnic tables are waiting for you to absorb the dazzling view.

After more than two miles of walking, the trail comes to a gate. There is also a trail marker for Ridgeline Trail with trail number 19 on it. Go through the gate and follow the trail downhill, first looping to the right and then to the left. The trail name becomes Thermalito Trail. Stay on this trail for almost three miles as it climbs up and down along the top of deep Kilkare canyon to the west. This is not only the quietest most remote part of the trail but also the shadiest.

After passing several intersecting trails, turn left onto Ridgeline Trail again. It climbs a couple of short hills for a little over a half mile. Turn right onto Oak Tree Trail then look carefully for the sign for Woodland Trail, a narrow footpath. Turn right and follow it downhill to Oak Tree Trail. Turn right and return to the parking lot.

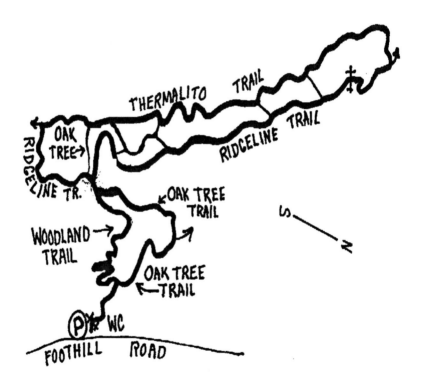

Sunol Regional Wilderness

Overview

The drive along Calaveras Road to Sunol is a good indication of the beauty that lies ahead. The narrow winding road follows the canyon floor under a canopy of oaks and leads to the small kiosk at the park entrance. From here begin endless trails that wind up and down hills, cross creeks, pass through shady oak and madrone forests, and cling to the sides of hills on small paths. Outstanding views are everywhere in Sunol, whether it be San Francisco Bay, Calaveras and San Antonio Reservoirs, or distant peaks.

Native Americans were the first to view this land and found it a resourceful place to live. The area provided the natural resources they needed to survive: water, food, shelter, protection. Today's visitor can see remnants of this early settlement in the on-site museum or by a docent-lead tour. In more recent years, ranchers lived and ranched here. Still today, it is not unusual to come across grazing cattle straddling hiking trails and drinking from the creeks.

Sunol's 7000 acres are crisscrossed by many creeks, mostly seasonal except the largest, Alameda Creek. These waterways, enhancing the feeling of isolation, are the special trademark of this park. The most popular place along Alameda Creek is "Little Yosemite", so named because of the tumbling boulders that dam and release the water into mini waterfalls. These creeks nourish many examples of native oaks, willow and sycamore, and provide excellent birding opportunities.

Spring is a stunning season in this park, with blankets of green grassland and many varieties of wildflowers. Poppies, lupine, paintbrush, milkmaid and monkey flower among others, carpet vast areas in blue, yellow, red and orange.

Be sure to end your hike with a picnic at one of Sunol's shaded picnic tables and cool your feet in the creek flowing close by. The kids can skip rocks and wade while you relax under the shady embrace of sycamore trees and tune in to the rippling sound of Alameda Creek.

Sunol Regional Wilderness

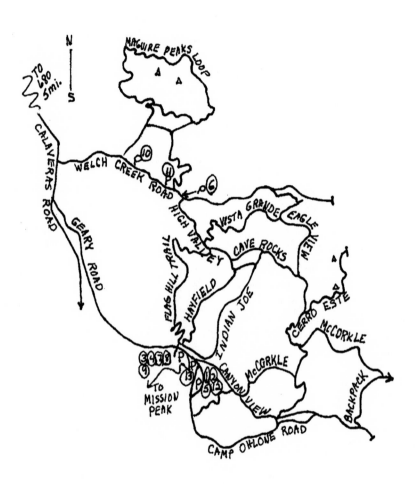

Note that all directions are from the intersection of Highways 580 and 680.

Welch Creek Road entrance: Drive South on 680 and exit at Calaveras Road/Highway 84. Turn left onto Calaveras Road. After approximately 3 miles, turn left onto Welch Creek Road.

Main Sunol entrance: Follow the directions to the Welch Creek Road entrance. Continue past Welch Creek Road for another ¾ mile and look carefully for the Geary Road sign on the left. Turn left and follow Geary Road into the park.

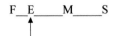
Sunol Regional Wilderness: Hike 1
Little Yosemite

Little Yosemite is aptly named for its creeks, boulders, and cascades. Don't expect the spectacular waterfalls of its namesake park, but it is quite pretty nonetheless. Most of the year, the creek will be grand enough to give hikers the sensation that they are somewhere else, perhaps in the Sierras. On those hot summer days, enjoy the pools and babbling creek. The trail climbs only slightly, making a great afternoon stroll for new hikers and for those towing kids.

Highlights:
- ❖ Year round creek
- ❖ Mini waterfalls
- ❖ Native Sycamore trees
- ❖ Large climbing boulders
- ❖ Good kid's hike

Trail Details:
Distance: 2.2 miles
Time: 1 hour
Altitude Gain: 200'

Trail Map: East Bay Regional Park District – Sunol

Getting there: Go to the main Sunol entrance. After passing the kiosk, continue to the last parking lot at the end of the road.

The trail: Go through the gate at the end of the parking lot and continue across the bridge. Follow Camp Ohlone Road, as it parallels Alameda Creek. Alternatively, drop down closer to the creek on the smaller unmarked footpath accessed to the right at the end of the bridge. However, the footing is somewhat unstable and the paths have a way of disappearing with seasonal rain and erosion. Return to the main trail. When you get to Little Yosemite, walk off the trail to the right to get a good view. This offers lots of welcome shade on a hot day.

Retrace your steps back to the parking lot.

Option: Instead of turning around, continue on Camp Ohlone Road to the end of the park. You will see one of the largest groves of native Sycamore trees in northern California. This happens because, as the creek bed levels, it spreads out into a small plain, a great natural irrigation system for the thirsty sycamores. Return on Camp Ohlone road to the parking area. This option adds one mile and about 200 feet elevation gain.

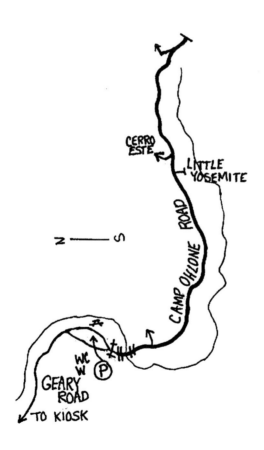

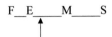

Sunol Regional Wilderness: Hike 2
Canyon View Trail

This short pleasant trail is fittingly named. It begins on a wide gravel road then circles back on a narrow trail perched over Alameda Creek and the canyon below. It's scenic and easy enough for the beginning hiker, as the climb is gradual. For a more aerobic alternative, reverse the direction. That way there is an early uphill climb, followed by an easy downhill.

Highlights:
- ❖ "Little Yosemite"
- ❖ Canyon views
- ❖ Good kid's hike
- ❖ Picnic area
- ❖ Wildflowers

Trail Details:
Distance: 2.6 miles
Time: 1 hour
Altitude Gain: 400'

Trail Map: East Bay Regional Park District – Sunol

Getting there: Go to the main Sunol entrance. After passing the kiosk, continue to the last parking lot at the end of the road.

The trail: Walk to the end of the parking lot, go through the gate and cross the bridge. This is Camp Ohlone Road and follows Alameda Creek.

In the spring, the hillside to the left of Camp Ohlone Road is covered with orange sticky monkey flowers and purple deadly nightshade, creating quite a sight! After a mile on this road, walk to one of the canyon overlooks on the right to get a good view of "Little Yosemite," a mini version of its famous namesake.

Just beyond this sight, turn left onto Canyon View Trail, another good spot for wildflowers. This narrow trail meanders parallel to the road and climbs slightly, and overlooks the canyon and creek; watch for detour overlook paths to the left. Turn left on

McCorkle Trail. At the bottom of the hill, the trail turns sharply right and leads to a gate. Go through the gate, walk a few steps and turn right on Camp Ohlone Road. This crosses the bridge and leads back to the parking area.

Option: Pass the first turn to Canyon View and continue another .4 miles to a second Canyon View Trail access point on the left. This connects with the other portion of the trail described above. If you get to the "W" tree you have gone too far. This option adds .7 miles and 100' elevation gain to the hike.

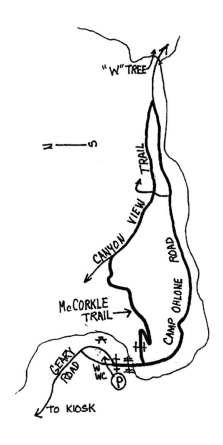

Sunol Regional Wilderness: Hike 3
Cave Rocks

This is a perfect hike for hikers of all ages. It isn't too steep, and the reward is an impressive set of boulders that aren't really caves but are lots of fun for kids to climb. On the way to the "caves," youngsters can dabble in the creek when it's flowing, or look for wildflowers along the edge.

Highlights:
- ❖ Great kids' destination
- ❖ Babbling creek
- ❖ Plenty of shade

Trail Detail:
Distance: 2.8 miles
Time: 1½ hours
Altitude Gain: 700'

Trail Map: East Bay Regional Park District – Sunol

Getting there: Go to the main Sunol entrance. Continue past the kiosk. Park in the first parking area after the visitor center on the left, near the bridge that crosses Alameda Creek.

The trail: Cross the bridge at the left end of the parking area, and turn right. After a few minutes, watch for the Indian Joe Creek Trail signpost and turn left. This is a very pleasant trail that follows a creek lined with Sycamore and Oak trees and native creek vegetation. In the winter, watch for popcorn plants, easily identified by their blooms that resemble popcorn.

Depending on your young hikers, you will reach Cave Rocks in 30 to 50 minutes. Watch for the boulders on the left and then take time to climb and enjoy these impressive formations. The boulders are small enough for young climbers to scramble on.

Return the way you came getting a new view of this beautiful creek on the easy hike down. Turn right at the end of the trail, and cross the bridge back to the parking area.

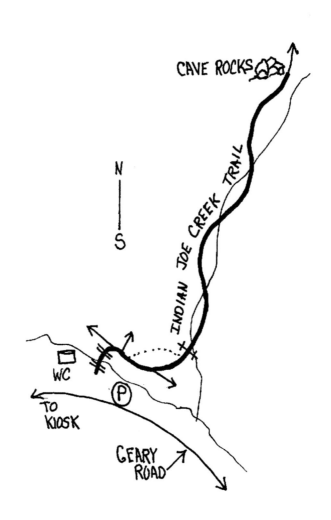

CAVE ROCKS

INDIAN JOE CREEK TRAIL

N
S

WC

TO
KIOSK

P

GEARY
ROAD

Sunol Regional Wilderness: Hike 4
Indian Joe Creek Trail

This is a popular trail for Sunol hikers and it's easy to see why. It follows a feeder creek that flows down a narrow canyon and empties into Alameda Creek. A variety of water loving native trees hug the creek and canyon sides bringing shady relief on a sunny day. The climb is steady but mostly gradual. In 30 to 45 minutes, the trail flattens out as it intersects Cave Rocks Road. The rest is downhill.

Highlights:
- ❖ Shade
- ❖ Seasonal creek
- ❖ Aerobic workout
- ❖ Wildflowers

Trail Details:
Distance: 3.8 miles
Time: 1¾ hours
Altitude Gain: 800'

Trail Map: East Bay Regional Park District – Sunol

Getting there: Go to the main Sunol entrance. Continue past the kiosk, and park in the first parking area after the visitor center on the left, near the bridge that crosses Alameda Creek.

The trail: Cross the bridge at the left end of the parking area, and turn right. Follow the path along Alameda Creek to Indian Joe Creek Trail. Turn left and follow the narrow path uphill for almost a mile, crossing the creek along the way. The trail passes Cave Rocks so the kids (or the kid in you!) may want to stop and climb the magnificent boulders.

At the end of the trail, turn left on Cave Rocks Road; after a short distance enjoy the year-round pond on the right. Turn left again at the High Valley/Hayfield Road sign onto Hayfield Road. Follow this trail to its end and turn right. Turn left at the bridge and return to the parking area.

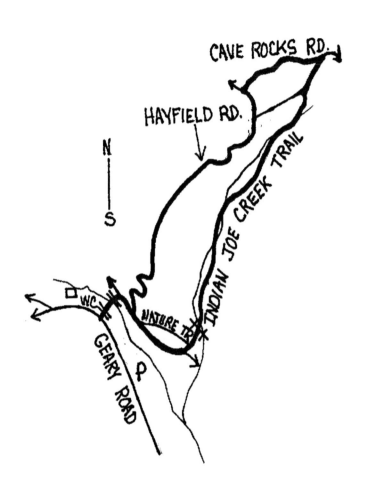

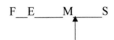

Sunol Regional Wilderness: Hike 5
High Valley Loop

This is a "top of the world' hike. Throughout most of the hike expansive views overlook much of the park with Maguire Peaks and Calaveras Reservoir as a backdrop. There is a covered picnic area half way through the hike next to an historical old barn. An option to Flag Hill will make this a more strenuous hike.

Highlights:
❖ Panoramic views
❖ Picnic area
❖ Ponds and creeks
❖ Wildflowers

Trail Details:
Distance: 3.8 miles
Time: 2 hours
Altitude Gain: 1050'

Trail Map: East Bay Regional Park District – Sunol

Getting there: Go to the Welch Creek Road entrance and park on the right side of the road, approximately 1¼ mile from the turnoff (shortly after the lower Maguire Peaks trailhead on the left). Note there is only space for two cars.

The trail: High Valley Trail starts on the right side of Welch Creek Road. It begins as a short climb with a few switchbacks, shaded by native oak trees. When the trail comes out into the open, turn left on Vista Grande Road. Don't forget to turn around and capture the view of Calaveras Reservoir and Maguire Peaks as you climb up this hill.

Bear right on Eagle View Road and enjoy more views of the interior of the park as they unfold. Descend to a shady creek and then out into the open again. Turn right onto Cave Rocks Road. This bears right and becomes High Valley Road and leads to the old barn and picnic area.

To complete the hike, continue on High Valley Road and go through the gate to the stone monument. Bear right, staying on High Valley Road and return to Welch Creek Road.

Option: To get to Flag Hill, from the stone monument look to the left and a little behind you to the gate leading to Flag Hill Trail. Go through the gate and follow the trail to the end. Enjoy the view and retrace your steps back to the stone monument and follow the directions above. This option increases the hike to 7.8 miles and a total gain of 1350'.

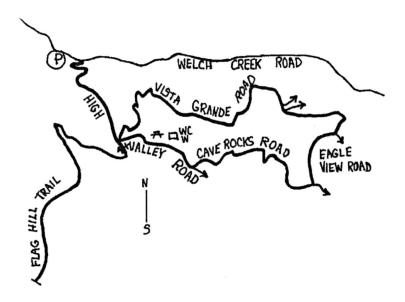

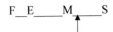

Sunol Regional Wilderness: Hike 6
Flag Hill Trail

This hike is full of magnificent scenery and has a little history as well. The old road leads to what remains of an old ranching homestead. The red barn and ice cellar are all that is left but a new added covered picnic area makes this a good destination hike. The climb to Flag Hill is gradual and worth the effort as the view from the top shows off the lush lower valley. Enjoy descending on the narrow path to the bottom of the hill while gazing at a variety of native wildflowers during the late winter and spring months.

Highlights:
- ❖ Hilltop view
- ❖ Historical site
- ❖ Wild flowers
- ❖ Halfway picnic area

Trail Details:
Distance: 3.9 miles
Time: 2 hours
Altitude Gain: 1100'

Trail Map: East Bay Regional Park District – Sunol

Getting there: Go to the main Sunol entrance. Continue past the kiosk. Park past the visitor center on the left, near the bridge that crosses Alameda Creek.

The trail: Cross the bridge at the left end of the parking area, turn right and then left onto Hayfield Road. This is the old ranch road that leads up to the barn and picnic area. After a steady uphill climb, and just before reaching High Valley Road, look to the left for a view of a large patch of cactus, obviously not native. There is quite a show in late summer when it is in full bloom.

Turn left on High Valley Road and walk the short distance to the barn and picnic area. Enjoy a rest and then proceed along the road in the same direction until you come to a stone monument with trail signs. To the left, beyond the large Eucalyptus tree,

164

there is a gate that leads to Flag Hill. Go through the gate and stay on the trail until it ends on a cliff with a dazzling overlook of the Alameda Creek valley.

Retrace the path on the ridge top a few hundred feet to a trail marker with "to park headquarters," and "Shady Glen Trail" on it. Turn right and switch back and forth down this narrow path, going through a couple of gates, to the bottom of the hill. Notice the long -blooming wildflowers in season on the way down. At the bottom of the hill, continue straight along the creek, turn right onto the bridge and return to the parking area.

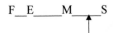

Sunol Regional Park: Hike 7
Backpack Trail

This is one of the most beautiful spring hikes in the Tri-Valley. It is also a little-traveled area of the park, revealing unspoiled pastureland, secluded valleys and rock filled creeks. A large portion of this hike follows the Ohlone Wilderness Trail. There isn't a lot of shade along the trail, so it is best to avoid the midday heat of summer.

Highlights:
- ❖ Spring wildflowers
- ❖ Canyon vista
- ❖ Calaveras Reservoir view
- ❖ Little Yosemite
- ❖ Sandstone outcroppings

Trail Details:
Distance: 6¼ miles
Time: 3 hours
Altitude Gain: 1250'

Trail Map: East Bay Regional Park District – Sunol

Getting there: Go to the main Sunol entrance. Park in the farthest lot, Alameda Grove, about ½ mile after the kiosk.

The trail: Walk to the end of the parking onto Camp Ohlone Road. Turn left after crossing the bridge onto McCorkle Trail (the trail sign is set back from the road). After .6 mile turn right onto Canyon View Trail for another .6 mile. Then turn left on Cerro Este Trail. This will meet another leg of McCorkle Trail; turn right.

Most of the climbing is now done. Follow McCorkle Trail until it comes to a large oak tree on the right with limbs resting on the ground forming a perfect picnic bench! On the other side of the trail, look for seeping spring monkey flowers during springtime-spectacular yellow wildflowers that thrive in the damp soil.

The trail crosses "Rock Scramble", a creek that can be impassable after a heavy rain. Mostly, it is a beautiful rock cascade, easily crossed. Continue on the trail to Backpack Road that leads down to Camp Ohlone Road.

Turn right and look for the famous "W" tree on the right side of the trail. It is a large sycamore tree shaped much like its namesake. After about 10 minutes, the trail passes "Little Yosemite" tumbling down Alameda Creek. Follow the road back to the parking lot.

Option: Reverse the direction, and you won't believe it is the same hike. The views are entirely new!

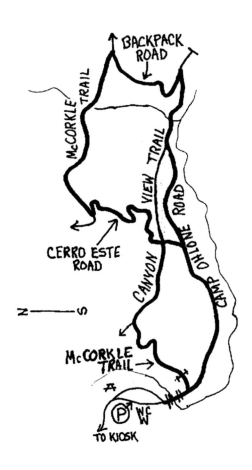

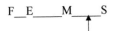
Sunol Regional Wilderness: Hike 8
Vista Grande

This is one of several trails in Sunol that follows a beautiful creek bed. Eventually the trail narrows and hugs a hillside full of spring wildflowers that leads to Vista Grande, a spectacular view that shows off the wonder of this park. A picnic area at the old red barn is a good place to relax before the trek down.

Highlights:
❖ Seasonal creeks
❖ Panoramic views
❖ Picnic area
❖ Spring wildflowers

Trail Details:
Distance: 4.8 miles
Time: 2¼ hours
Altitude Gain: 1500'

Trail Map: East Bay Regional Park District – Sunol

Getting there: Go to the main Sunol entrance. Continue past the kiosk. Park in the first parking area after the visitor center on the left, near the bridge that crosses Alameda Creek.

The trail: Cross the bridge at the left end of the parking area, then bear right. After a quarter mile, turn left on Indian Joe Creek Trail. Follow it for a mile as it climbs along a beautiful creek bed, crosses it and continues to the intersection of Cave Rocks Road. Turn right and after a short climb, pass Eagle View Road. Shortly, turn left on Eagle View Trail.

The trail dips into a shady ravine with a tumbling waterfall in the rainy season. It then climbs very gradually, clinging to the hillside. In springtime, there is a lush wildflower display of Lupine and Poppy. The trail continues to a stone monument that identifies Vista Grande, or "big view," aptly named for the expansive panoramic view.

Continue on Vista Grande Road and turn left on High Valley Road. You will see the old barn and picnic area, a good place for a rest. Turn right on Hayfield Road, follow it down to the creek, turn right, cross the bridge and return to the parking area.

Option: From the barn, walk back to the large eucalyptus tree where Vista Grande meets High Valley. Look beyond the tree to the left. There is a gate that leads to Flag Hill Road. Go through the gate and follow the trail to its end, about one mile. Return to High Valley Trail and follow the directions above back to the parking area. This option adds 2¼ miles and 300' altitude.

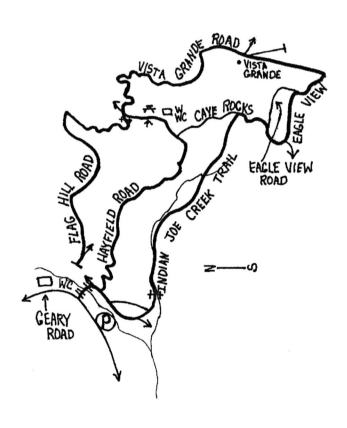

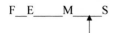

Sunol Regional Wilderness: Hike 9
McCorkle Loop Trail

This trail is a favorite of hikers, because it covers most of the central section of the park and reveals much of the landscape variety for which Sunol is known. At first, the trail meanders along a beautiful creek with lots of shade and rock out-croppings. It then opens up to grassland with many ponds that keep the numerous cattle watered. This hike is all uphill the first half, and all downhill the second, so there is a good steady workout as well.

Highlights:

❖ Creek side trail
❖ Good workout
❖ Mountaintop views

Trail Details:

Distance: 4.9 miles
Time: 3½ hours
Altitude Gain: 1400'

Trail Map: East Bay Regional Park District – Sunol

Getting there: Go to the main Sunol entrance. Continue past the kiosk. Park in the first parking area after the visitor center on the left, near the bridge that crosses Alameda Creek.

The trail: Cross the bridge at the left end of the parking area, then bear right. After a quarter mile, turn left on Indian Joe Creek Trail. Follow it for a mile as it climbs along a beautiful creek bed, crosses it and continues to the intersection of Cave Rocks Road. Turn right and after an uphill climb in open country, the trail reaches the Cerro Este stone monument. Enjoy the breathtaking view of the park, the surrounding hills and Calaveras Reservoir.

With your back to Cave Rocks Road, bear right onto Cerro Este, going downhill and passing a couple of cow ponds along the way. Turn right onto McCorkle Trail and follow it mostly downhill. After a sharp right turn, begin watching for the small Canyon View Trail sign. Turn right and stay on this trail as it drops to Alameda Creek, then passes Indian Joe Creek Trail. Turn left at the bridge and return to the parking area.

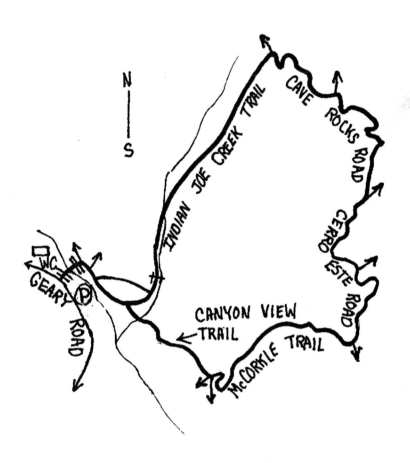

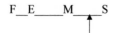
Sunol Regional Wilderness: Hike 10
Lower Maguire Peaks

In about one hour you can hike to the top of Maguire Peaks (1688' elevation) and have a magnificent 360-degree view of local parklands, Calaveras and San Antonio Reservoirs, and the San Francisco Bay. The last part of the climb is quite steep, but the view is worth every step.

Highlights:	Trail Details:
❖ 360 degree view at the top	Distance: 4.6 miles
❖ Shady creek	Time: 2 hours
❖ Cardiovascular climb to peak	Altitude Gain: 1250'

Trail Map: East Bay Regional Park District – Sunol

Getting there: Go to the Welch Creek Road park entrance. The trailhead is about ¾ mile up the road on the left. Parking is limited to 3 or 4 cars.

The trail: The trail starts as a narrow footpath that follows a shady creek; metal arrows are positioned periodically to mark the trail. Watch for poison oak on this trail. After about 15 minutes the trail bears left at a trough. Follow the arrows and carefully watch for the one that directs you to the right. This leads to Maguire Peaks Loop, a wide road. Turn left.

After about 10 minutes on this trail, it curves to the right. Immediately look for a very narrow unmarked footpath on the right leading steeply up the side of the hill to the peak. If you can't find it, look up and find the trail near the top of the peak. Follow the trail down with your eyes to locate the beginning. Climb the steep hill and enjoy the views along the way. When you have reached the top, go right and enjoy a snack and the view on the well-placed boulders.

Note: If you don't find the trail going up to the peak, just continue straight on Maguire Peaks Loop, pass the bench on the right and follow the directions below, starting with the fourth sentence.

Take the only other trail down which is on the northwest side of the peak. At the bottom of the descent there is a bench. Turn right onto Maguire Peaks Loop. When you come to an intersection with a left turn, pass it by and continue on the Loop. In about 20 minutes you will reach an intersection with a sign for Maguire Peaks Loop. Pass this and shortly turn right on the next road. After about 5 minutes you will see an old stone culvert on the right. Directly opposite is a narrow footpath. Follow this to an open grassy area, under some oak trees, and connect to Lower Maguire Peaks Trail that returns to Welch Creek Road.

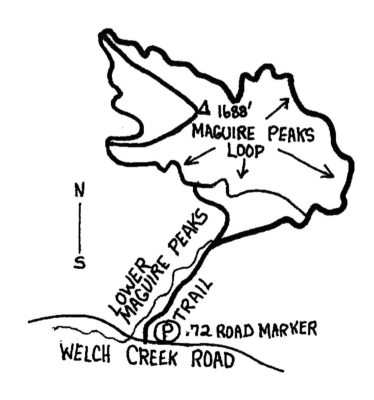

173

Sunol Regional Wilderness: Hike 11
Upper Maguire Trail

This is one of the least used trails in Sunol. This remote trail provides hillside walking with views of the interior hills and canyons of Sunol. There are outstanding views of the park, reservoirs and Bay area as this trail joins the more popular Maguire Peaks Trail and climbs the peak. Watch late blooming wildflowers on the north side of the loop trail.

Highlights:	**Trail Details:**
❖ Secluded trail	Distance: 5.9 miles
❖ Expansive views	Time: 3 hours
❖ Aerobic workout	Altitude Gain: 1300'

Trail Map: East Bay Regional Park District – Sunol

Getting there: Go to the Welch Creek Road entrance. The trail is difficult to find. Drive up the road and watch for the mileage markers. The parking area for this trail is on the left at the 1.6 mile marker.

The Trail: Get onto the marked hard-to-see footpath that crosses a tiny creek and continues into the canyon straight ahead. A short distance into the canyon, the trail switches back and begins to climb as it clings to the side of a steep hillside. It is very rough and uneven so watch your footing.

The trail flattens out and intersects with Maguire Peak Trail. Turn right, then pass the first unmarked road on the left and turn left at the next road; this is Maguire Peaks Loop. The trail descends a little and makes a hairpin left under a small group of oaks, then begins to climb and curve right. After the second big turn to the right, watch for a narrow trail hidden in the tall grass on the right that climbs up to Maguire Peak. If you look further

174

up the hill, the trail will be visible and will help to locate its beginning.

Follow this trail straight up to the top of the peak. When you have reached the top, go to the right and rest on the boulders and enjoy the view.

Note: If you don't find the trail going up to the peak, just continue straight on Maguire Peaks Loop, pass the bench on the right and follow the directions below, starting with the third sentence.

Descend on the small path on the northwest down to the main loop trail where there is a bench. Turn right. The trail follows the base of the two peaks, circling to the right. Do not take the first left turn; it comes to a dead end. Continue on Maguire Peak Trail, avoiding any right turns. Eventually, the trail descends slightly into a dense grove of oak trees and then climbs into open grassland. Watch carefully for the trail marker for Upper Peaks Trail on the left as it is not obvious. Follow this trail back to the parking area.

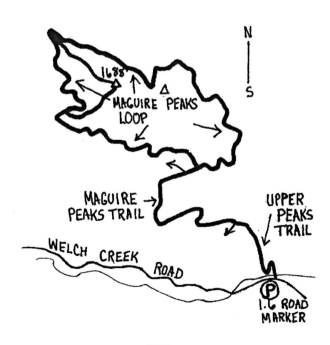

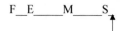
Sunol Regional Wilderness: Hike 12
Cerro Este Trail

Only by flying in a plane could the view from this hike be enhanced. Standing at one mountaintop vantage point, you can see almost the entire park. To get to this point, the trail goes up and up almost without relief for an hour and a half. The payoff is this gorgeous panoramic view! This is a great winter hike; in the summer leave early to avoid the unrelenting sun, as there are few trees shading the trail. The return is a delight with uninterrupted downhill hiking and a bonus view of Little Yosemite gorge.

Highlights:
* Panoramic views
* Lengthy aerobic workout
* Downhill return

Trail Details:
Distance: 6.2 miles
Time: 3 ½ hours
Altitude Gain: 2000'

Trail Map: East Bay Regional Park District – Sunol

Getting there: Go to the main Sunol entrance and continue straight to Alameda Grove, the farthest parking lot.

The trail: Walk to the end of the parking lot, go through the gate and cross the bridge. Immediately, turn left on McCorkle Trail and begin climbing. Stay on McCorkle for almost two miles. Turn left on Cerro Este Road and continue climbing for another mile and a quarter, passing a couple of stone monument trail markers along the way. Look up the trail; there are two rounded peaks. This is the goal.

Continue walking up the trail, passing the first peak. Proceed to the second peak for expansive views of Mission Peak, Apperson Ridge, Maguire Peaks, and Calaveras Reservoir. Many of the lower hills are visible from this vantage point, as is the red barn down on High Valley Trail. After enjoying the view and the breeze, descend on the same trail but pass McCorkle Trail and instead turn right on Canyon View Trail. This is a narrow path that follows the hill over Little Yosemite gorge. Take a little detour on one of the paths to the left for an overlook. Tread carefully to not trample the colorful wildflowers in the spring. Turn left on McCorkle Trail (the trail marker can be hard to see) and follow it down to the bridge and the parking area.

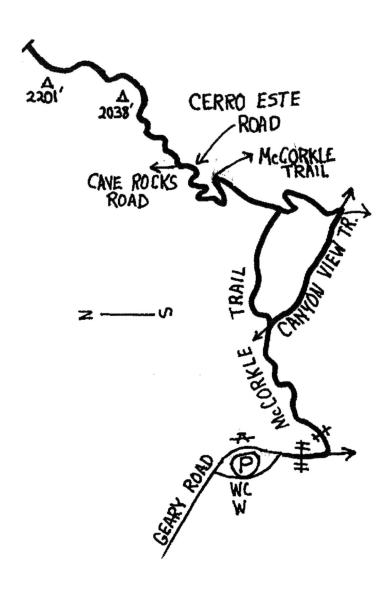

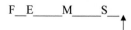

Sunol Regional Wilderness: Hike 13
Mission Peak Trail

This is one of those very special trails in the Bay region. It offers 360-degree views from Mount Tamalpais all the way to Mount Hamilton. The entire bay is visible on a clear day, as well as the bridges and the surrounding metropolis. The long gradual uphill becomes a pleasant five-mile downhill return..

Highlights:
* Panoramic views
* Good workout
* Fall color
* Half shade

Trail Details:
Distance: 9.6 miles
Time: 4 ½ hours
Altitude Gain: 2300'

Trail Map: East Bay Regional Park District – Mission Peak

Getting there: Go to the main Sunol park entrance. Park in the stable parking area shortly after the kiosk, on the right.

Permit Required: A permit is required for use of the Ohlone Wilderness Trail. Contact park headquarters for information and a map of Mission Peak Regional Preserve.

The trail: The trailhead begins just beyond the outhouses. Go through the gate onto a narrow path leading uphill, crossing Calaveras Road. The trail continues on the other side and widens into a road. This is the Ohlone Wilderness Trail, a long, but somewhat shady, climb to the base of Mission Peak.

Close to the top, at a dip into a grove of trees, pass the sign to Laurel Canyon Trail and continue to the base of the mountain. Turn left at Eagle Trail. This swings right and leads to Peak Trail and Mission Peak. Enjoy a picnic and the view! Continue down the other side of the peak and turn right on Eagle Trail and left on Ohlone Wilderness Trail. Now enjoy the several miles of downhill hiking to the parking area

Option: From the main road, turn left on Laurel Canyon Trail. This is a shady downhill trek. Cross the often muddy creek and continue along the fence as it turns right, then opens onto the main trail. This adds .8 miles and 20 minutes to this hike.

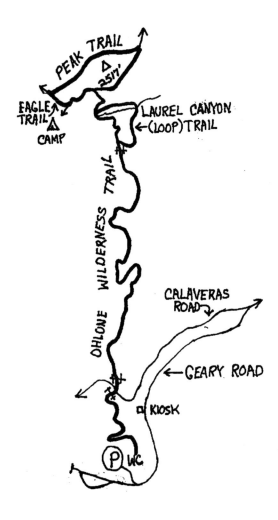

Sycamore Grove Regional Park

Overview

Those who live in Livermore try to keep this gem a secret. It's not that they don't want to share it, it's that they want the park to keep its rural feeling, as it has for over a hundred years. This old ranch has history, wildlife, agriculture, and lots of trees. It is no surprise that one can hike almost entirely in shade, as Sycamore Grove has one of the largest stands of native sycamore trees in California. The huge leaves provide cover for the many birds and animals that make Sycamore Grove their home: great horned owls, snowy egrets, deer, bobcat and great blue heron to name a few. In early morning and late afternoon, the whistles, caws, and chirps are a natural symphony.

The original, and lower section of the park has several miles of trails that are completely flat. A paved 2½ mile trail connects this park with Veterans Park. However, to take advantage of the almost year round creek where most of the birds forage, walk along one of the unpaved paths. Not only are these paths quieter and less used, but they are also shaded by sycamore trees.

The relatively new section of the park, previously cattle grazing country, gives some altitude to the hiking. Climb up any of the trails and see expansive views of Livermore. This high vantage point also reveals the layout of the historical Olivina Ranch, an important landmark for Livermore. Another trail leads to a preserved riparian area tucked in a back corner of the park, and a couple of others are being studied for restoration.

Over a hundred years ago, the Smith family built their house and winery at the end of one of the two tree lined avenues. They planted orchards, vineyards and olive groves and made their own wine in an old brick winery. The house burned down but the winery structure remains. Livermore planners had the foresight to preserve the land and history for the benefit of us all.

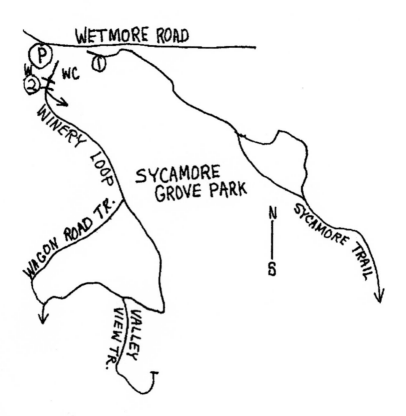

Directions to Sycamore Grove Regional Park:

Take 580 east. Take the North Livermore exit and turn right at the light. Turn right onto Fourth Street, then left onto L Street. L Street becomes Arroyo Road. Turn right onto Wetmore. The park entrance is on the left.

Sycamore Grove Regional Park: Hike 1
Sycamore Trail

This walk is close to town, and yet it seems far from civilization. The trail stays flat through old farmland so even timid hikers will enjoy this outing. It is shaded with one of the largest stands of sycamore trees in California, and close to a perennial creek. At times you might see deer, great horned owls, hawks, egrets and other water fowl. In spring, long green grasses and wildflowers carpet the ground under the trees. Birders frequent this area for the variety of birds nesting in the large sycamores.

Highlights:
- ❖ Sycamore trees
- ❖ Creek
- ❖ Wildlife
- ❖ Nature trail

Trail Details:
Distance: 4 ¼ miles
Time: 1 ½ hours
Altitude Gain: negligible

Trail Map: Livermore Area Parks and Recreation District - Sycamore Grove

Getting there: Park in the Sycamore Grove parking lot.

The trail: From the parking lot, walk towards the main paved trail but instead of taking it, bear left just after the kiosk onto the unpaved Sycamore Trail (see note below). This trail skirts a vineyard for a while and then turns right under an alley of trees. At the end of the trees, turn left and continue straight. After 5-10 minutes turn right and then shortly turn left before the trail crosses the creek, staying on Sycamore Trail.

The trail now meanders under a large grove of oak and sycamore trees where deer are often spotted. Follow this for a little over a half mile until it comes to a bridge. Turn around and retrace your steps until the trail forks. Turn right and continue until this loop connects to the main trail. Follow this back to the starting point.

Note: Some trails do not have trail signs.

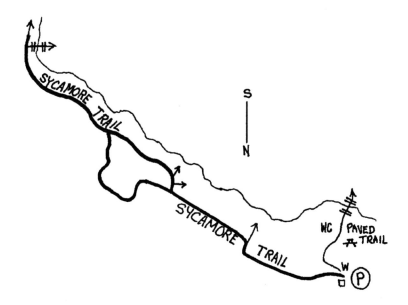

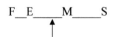

Sycamore Grove Regional Park: Hike 2
Valley View Trail

This trail leads into the newest acquisition of Sycamore Grove Park. It follows the original wine harvest road that the Smith family used to access their gravitation fed grape crusher. It passes by the second home site for the Smith family and then climbs to the highest point in the park for an expansive view of Livermore, Dublin and Mount Diablo. This is old ranch country, quite barren due to extensive grazing, so there is little shade.

Highlights:	Trail Details:
❖ Rural park close to town	Distance: 3½ miles
❖ Historical interest	Time: 1¾ hours
❖ Valley views	Altitude Gain: 650'

Trail Map: Livermore Area Parks and Recreation District - Sycamore Grove

Getting there: Park in the Sycamore Grove parking lot.

The trail: Get on the paved trail. After the trail crosses a bridge, it forks. Take the right turn onto the unpaved Winery Loop Trail (see note below) and follow it around the perimeter of the park, passing the Park Ranger's house on the right and Olivina Trail on the left. Soon the trail splits in four directions. Two of the trails bear right up into the hilly part of the park. The trail you are on continues straight ahead. Take the left of the two uphill trails and continue under a tunnel of old olive trees. A point of historical interest is the old wine chute visible as a slight depression at the top of the hill next to the fence.

On the left side of the trail are two old stonewalled pits that were allegedly Mrs. Smith's fishponds. On the right, beyond the palms, is the former second home site for the same family. The trail turns right after the eucalyptus trees. Turn left at the next fork, onto Valley View Trail.

Follow this trail uphill along the gully. It levels out a couple of times and climbs again. Turn left at the top of the hill; the trail ends at a fence with an outstanding view of the whole valley. To reach the highest point in the park turn right at the top of the hill instead of left, and climb two more short hills. You will be rewarded with a 360-degree view.

Return downhill on the same trail. At the bottom of the hill turn left onto Wagon Road Trail. Stay on this trail as it curves right and leads back to the Winery Loop Trail. Turn left and follow this back to the parking lot.

Note: There may not be trail signs posted on the trails.

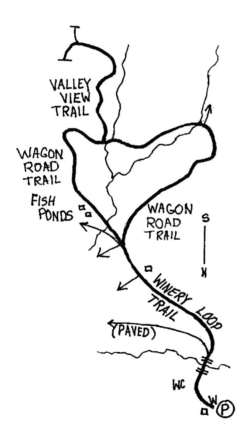

Happy trails!

From Nancy and Jacky

Nancy Rodrigue and Jacky Poulsen, authors

Nancy Rodrigue and Jacky Poulsen are long time Livermore residents. They have hiked the Tri-Valley hills extensively over the past 15 years. Their goal in writing this book is to share the amazing beauty and diverse hiking opportunities the area has to offer.

Barbara Mallon, photographer

LaVergne, TN USA
23 February 2011

217539LV00002B/1/P